ENVIRONMENTAL
SUPPLY CHAIN MANAGEMENT

Ram Narasimhan, Ph.D.
Professor of Operations Management
Eli Broad Graduate School of Management
Michigan State University

and

Joseph R. Carter, D.B.A., C.P.M.
National Association of Purchasing Management Professor
Supply Chain Management Program
Arizona State University

ACKNOWLEDGMENTS •

The Center for Advanced Purchasing Studies and the authors would like to thank the participating companies who served as case study sites for this research project. We thank these companies for their time and assistance: 3M Corporation; Daimler Benz, AG; Dekra Umwelt Gmbh; DENSO Manufacturing Michigan Inc; Eli Lilly; Grundfos; Hoechst AG; Honda of America Manufacturing; Novartis (formerly Ciba-Geigy); Novo Nordisk; Oscorna; Sidler GMBH and Co.; UZIN Georg Utz Gmbh & Co.; and Whirlpool Corporation.

Several industry purchasing executives reviewed the manuscript and provided many helpful suggestions for improving its content and presentation. Many thanks to:

    Anne Abney, Supply Manager, BellSouth Telecommunications, Inc.
    Lawrence Aldridge, Executive Director, Procurement Council, ARCO Procurement
    David T. Espenshade, Vice President, Director of Materials Management, Rohm and Haas Company

Finally, we would like to thank the members of the CAPS staff who have contributed to the completion of this study: Kerri Christiansen for her administrative assistance with the manuscript; Richard A. Boyle, Ph.D., Assistant Director; and Carol L. Ketchum, Assistant Director at CAPS, for carefully editing the manuscript and helping with the numerous administrative details that made the study possible; and Phillip L. Carter, D.B.A., Director of CAPS, for his encouragement, guidance, and support.

Of course, complete responsibility for the final study rests with the authors of this report.

ISBN: 0-945968-33-7

TABLE OF CONTENTS •

FIGURES AND APPENDICES •

EXECUTIVE SUMMARY •

Environmental supply chain management consists of the purchasing function's involvement in activities that include reduction, recycling, reuse, and the substitution of materials. Despite the potentially important role that the purchasing function can play in a firm's environmental activities, little research has been performed to date that examines the factors that affect environmental supply chain management. The authors examined how intra- and inter-organizational factors both drive and constrain purchasing's involvement in environmental supply chain activities.

This CAPS study was commissioned as a "theory development" study aimed at examining environmental issues of relevance to supply chain management. Environmental supply chain management (ESCM) is an emerging field. The principal objectives of this project were to identify leading-edge practices and methodologies in ESCM, develop a process framework by which environmental issues are incorporated into supply chain management strategies, and to propose pertinent issues for purchasing executives to consider in the future based on current and projected trends relating to ESCM.

Lessons Learned From Selected Case Studies

In-depth case studies were the preferred method of information collection during this project. The authors spent at least one day at each case-study site discussing environmental supply chain management issues with a variety of senior and middle managers from each firm. The authors learned something of value from each case study; what follows is a brief synopsis of the key lessons learned from a representative selection of the case-study firms. We encourage the reader to examine each of the 14 case studies individually and thoroughly. A wealth of useful information is available.

The case study participants were:

3M Corporation
Daimler Benz, AG
Dekra Umwelt GmbH
DENSO Manufacturing Michigan, Inc.
Eli Lilly
Grundfos
Hoechst AG
Honda of America Manufacturing
Novartis (formerly, Ciba-Geigy)
Novo Nordisk
Oscorna

Sidler GMBH and Co.
UZIN Georg Utz Gmbh & Co.
Whirlpool Corporation

The key lessons learned from the case studies are summarized as follows:

- An early emphasis on environmental issues is important (3M started as early as in 1960!).

- Top management commitment to environmental issues is critical. For example, a separate environmental department reporting to the top management the importance attached to environmental issues by the company.

- Employee issues are an important part of becoming environmentally conscious. In 3M, employees are empowered to act in response to environmental problems, rather than simply offering suggestions. The reward structure also emphasizes results.

- Synergy between the company's strong environmental image and reputation, and environmentally sensitive products is important.

- A holistic approach, such as supply chain integration, to environmental management links reduction in energy consumption to waste generation and release of pollutants. Using a customer-driven environmental management system along with standard operating procedures facilitates supply chain integration.

- Setting aggressive and progressive environmental goals is important.

- Using tools such as life-cycle management (LCM) and environmental audits (EA) improves environmental and operating performance. Suppliers are asked to keep track of their cost of waste (COW) so that this can be reduced. Supplier negotiations and selection revolve around COW and other environmental issues.

- It is desirable to make early financial investment in environmental protection. Novartis was one of the first European companies to formulate environmental policies (1972).

6

- Top management commitment to environmental issues (as indicated by a high position for the environmental and safety department in an organization chart) is important to program success and commitment.

- Decentralization of environmental specialists in the different business units is most efficient.

- Environmental dimension should be viewed as an inseparable part of business performance. It is useful to set quantitative targets for different environmental performance measures.

- An initial strategy of speed to market followed by incremental changes in process designs that are environmentally friendly is important.

- A supply chain emphasis is required for optimizing environment value added (EVA) performance.

- An ability to tap emerging market suppliers for less sophisticated products as well as managing associative risks is important.

- A lean corporate environment group is desirable for expediting decision-making.

- Safe and environmentally responsible processes are important criteria for supplier selection.

- Supplier audits on environmental issues require a cross-functional initiative involving employees from quality assurance, environmental affairs and purchasing. Similarly, teams should include financial analysts who decide whether suppliers will be the most productive from the perspective of maximizing EVA make-or-buy decisions.

- Adherence of suppliers to quality and environment standards is a necessary prerequisite for achieving a company's objective of speed to market.

- Because of the long lead-times for new products, companies need to resort to early sourcing and early supplier involvement in basic product developmental work.

- Sourcing decisions must take into consideration safety issues, capacity of suppliers, and ability to treat compounds and effluents.

- Because of an emphasis on a lean group, purchasing has more responsibility to conduct timely supplier evaluations using criteria such as risk and environmental capability. This in turn affects the training and technical expertise expected of purchasing staff.

- Because of the emphasis on environmental value-added performance, companies turn to suppliers for use of their waste treatment facilities. Companies also seek to develop suppliers who can collect, clean and reship process waste back to the company.

- The range of influence for sourcing strategies and supplier identification is global.

- An experiential approach to environmental management as demonstrated by a considerably long history of environmental awareness is needed.

- A unique environmental performance system as indicated by the development of a customized composite index called Eco-productivity is needed.

- A proactive approach to environmental management as can be seen from the setting of specific targets for future environmental performance for outcomes, inputs, and processes is needed.

- An "open" approach of communicating environmental information to the general public is needed.

- Companies must carefully justify all environmental changes through either cost reduction or customer satisfaction issues.

- The focus of continuous improvement used so effectively during TQM program implementation can be applied quite effectively to improving environmental efficiency and effectiveness.

- The cross-functional relevance of environmental supply chain management is ensured by its direct impact on the supplier selection and management processes.

- Change should be viewed as a competitive tool and environmental efficiency viewed as a positive catalyst for change.

- Products and processes should be subjected to continual critical analysis at every stage of the value-added process.

- The early integration of suppliers into all decisions affecting them is critical to environmental effectiveness.

- The close alignment of supplier capabilities with buying firm environmental goals is critical to program success. This alignment can be achieved through an alliance supporting organizational and informational framework and the benchmarking of performance with environmental, quality, and cost parameters.

The case study results indicate the need for inter-functional coordination and the adoption of a value-chain perspective, including a closer interface between purchasing and other functions. Purchasing must interface with engineering to ensure that materials that are specified can be recycled or reused, or meet resource reduction goals.

The case studies yielded 16 themes relating to environmental supply chain management (see Chapter 5). The most important themes pursued by firms in this case study included: life-cycle management, environmental performance management, assessing supplier's environmental capability, and environmental auditing.

Projected Trends Relating To Environmentalism

While current trends affecting environmental manufacturing relate to re-manufacturing, reuse, process waste, human resource programs (such as empowerment, waste remediation teams, and employee suggestion programs), and inbound logistics, the future holds new trends that will change the face of environmental manufacturing. These trends are described as propositions:

Proposition 1: The level of consumer awareness of environmental issues will increase rapidly.

The influence of this trend can already be felt; consider the example of products relating to health care. Because of stringent product labeling standards and media exposure, there is considerable awareness among consumers of environmental topics that were heretofore "too technical."

Proposition 2: Firms will place an increasing emphasis on environmentalism in the evaluation of effectiveness of business processes.

Currently, there are several companies that use sophisticated environmental performance measurement schemes. This trend is expected to increase because an orientation toward business processes is common among most firms. Therefore, one can to assume that environmental issues should be considered at each business process level.

Proposition 3: The transfer of knowledge among subsidiaries of large firms will increase rapidly.

Firms will place an increasing emphasis on environmentalism in the evaluation of effectiveness of business processes through knowledge diffusion and uniform environmental standards.

Proposition 4: Four major inter-organizational forces will drive environmental supply chain activities. Those forces are governments, suppliers, customers, and competitors.

While the literature review suggests a set of internal and external drivers of environmental supply chain activities, this case research has provided a multi-variate empirical examination in order to identify which of these factors are the key driver(s) of environmental supply chain management activities.

Proposition 5: Upstream members of a supply chain will increasingly affect environmental supply chain activities, and purchasing managers will need to take action to manage these effects.

It is logical that a firm's customers, suppliers, and competitors, and its supply chain are affecting environmental supply chain management activities.

Proposition 6: As the quality of environmentally friendly inputs increases, greater will be the level of environmental supply chain management.

Increased vertical coordination through the supply chain will affect environmental purchasing activity. The case study data suggest that as vertical coordination increases, so too will the rate of adoption of new technology. While not all environmental supply chain management activities fall under the formal rubric of technologies, it is reasonable to consider the manner in which new environmental programs are adopted and implemented in a similar fashion. For example, the introduction of new environmentally efficient resources into the conversion process will require purchasing managers to act as coordinators of both process engineers and the suppliers of these resources.

Proposition 7: The greater the supply uncertainty, the greater the level of vertical coordination between buyers and suppliers.

The case study data suggest several propositions based upon the concept of environmental uncertainty. This proposition indicates that vertical coordination will in turn be positively correlated with the degree of supply uncertainty.

Summary

This research project found that environmental supply chain management strategies appear to be in their infancy stage. Even among the early adopters of environmental management, the majority seems to pursue environmental goals that avoid violations of environmental statutes and regulations. The use of proactive environmental programs as an aid to supplier selection and supplier quality assurance is distinctly lacking in importance. Purchasing also was found to have a major responsibility in implementation of a recycling strategy.

The environmental implications of purchasing activities on operational considerations and strategic considerations such as supply management and supply chain management was examined in this study. Three common purchasing practices that have the potential to undergo widespread change in the future due to environmental issues were identified. These were the identification of capable suppliers, domestic versus global sourcing, and the purchase of systems.

The accumulated evidence suggests that environmental supply chain issues will gain tremendous importance in the future. In Europe, trends toward environmental supply chain management are already visible. Although, an average U.S.-based firm may not be thinking along environmental issues while developing corporate strategy, pressures from global firms, including those based in the United States, are likely to influence other firms to follow the European trend.

Also, the results suggest a need to increase coordination with suppliers of environmentally friendly materials and technology, as well as with downstream channel members, including users and customers. The results also mandate the need for increased coordination and communication throughout the supply chain, as well as within the firm.

Conclusions

This research monograph summarized the key sourcing drivers for considering environmental issues, described several methods and tools, including company-specific methods, employed in several leading-edge firms, presented generic methodologies for important environmental tools, and offered implications for purchasing and supply chain management. The accumulated evidence suggests that environmental and, in particular, environmental supply chain management issues will gain tremendous importance in the future.

The results of this research were mixed in terms of the impact of environmental supply chain management issues on strategic purchasing decisions. While some leading-edge firms are successful in including environmental capability as a distinct criterion for evaluating suppliers, other firms do not seem to be giving the same amount of importance to environmental issues. Similarly, in leading-edge firms, new product development activities involve key suppliers at the earliest development stage. In fact, key suppliers are expected to contribute and eventually spearhead the design for environment initiatives for products developed by the buying firms.

The deployment strategy for sustainable development, which was extracted from the case data and presented in Chapter 4, suggests several roles for purchasing. In the future, purchasing executives need to be familiar with and use key environmental tools, such as life-cycle management and environmental auditing, which can affect the sourcing of materials and systems. Purchasing also needs to stay abreast of developments relating to innovative forms of environmentally sound packaging that can be used for inbound and outbound logistics. Future supplier development programs should include training modules for life-cycle cost assessment, environmental auditing of suppliers, and the use of pricing based on total cost of ownership.

A supply chain is often long and complex, consisting of several levels and dozens of members. Certainly, environmental issues occur at the second- and third-tier supplier levels. Conventional wisdom states that the entire supply chain should focus itself on the common goal of customer satisfaction. However, the complexity, length, and information inefficiencies of most chains make this focus somewhat distorted.

This report provides an empirical development of a practical model of environmental supply chain management, not a theory. The model can be viewed as the first stage of identifying and formulating the leading variables that affect environmental management of the supply chain. Thus, the purpose of the models presented in this report is to aid firms in systematically developing a managerial paradigm for the role of supply chain management in environmental endeavors. The results must therefore be considered developmental in nature, indicating the need for extension and replication.

While this research focused on inter-organizational factors that affect environmental supply chain management, the review of the literature indicated that intra-organizational factors have an influence in areas including a sincere commitment to environmental issues, successfully implemented ethical standards, the existence of managers who make a strong commitment and take personal responsibility for organizational adoption of an environmentally friendly philosophy, and the presence of adequate reward and incentive systems for employees.

Finally, an extension of this research can be used to consider the consequences of environmental supply chain management. What factors are in turn impacted by environmental purchasing activities and programs? A recent investigation by Klassen and McLaughlin found a positive link between environmental performance, measured in part by pollution emissions and quality awards, and financial performance. Extrapolating this research, it seems likely that the future will prove that environmental supply chain management, including environmental purchasing, affects environmental performance, and ultimately, financial performance.

What Follows

The following outcomes of this study are presented in subsequent chapters:

- A brief summary of the relevant management literature relating to environmental practices (Chapter 2).

- A description of practices currently being emphasized in a sample of firms in North America and Europe (Chapter 3).

- A description of the supply chain management themes resulting from these practices (Chapters 3 & 5).

- Detailed presentations of a select set of environmental supply chain management tools and practices (Chapter 4).

- A framework and a process by which environmental issues can be incorporated into supply chain management strategies (Chapter 6).

- A proposal of pertinent issues for purchasing executives to consider in the future based on current and projected trends relating to environmentalism (Chapter 6).

CHAPTER 1: INTRODUCTION •

Environmental issues are important to American firms. Companies in the United States now spend more than $124 billion annually complying with a myriad of environmental regulations (Kellogg, 1994). At the same time, the market for environmentally friendly products has increased to more than $200 billion (Shrivastava and Hart, 1994). In addition, the introduction of the ISO 14000 standard will increase firms' awareness of and involvement in environmental activities by not only providing an overall performance evaluation of a firm's environmental activities but also guiding managers in conducting life cycle analysis and environmental labeling of products (Tibor and Feldman, 1996).

Environmental issues are of interest not only to business in general but also to purchasing managers in particular. In a 1995 survey, purchasing managers' second highest-rated future concern was the impact of environmental regulation on purchasing activities (Monczka and Trent, 1995). This study involved a large sample of purchasing managers to examine the purchasing function's role in environmental activities, a concept that was termed *environmental purchasing*.

In this report, environmental purchasing is defined as the purchasing function's involvement in supply chain management activities in order to facilitate recycling, reuse, substitution, and resource reduction. As an example, buyers at Patagonia Company, after a careful analysis of the supply chain, identified several sources of environmentally friendly inputs, then worked with engineering to design fleece outerwear made from cheaper, environmentally sensitive, recycled products. Other examples of consumer products containing recycled inputs include automobiles (Ford), tissue paper (Northern), appliances (Black & Decker), and footwear (Nike).

Firms can reduce resources by manufacturing products that are easily recycled and reused; this can be achieved through methods such as using fewer materials, screwing or snapping components together instead of welding them, and creating inks that can be easily separated from paper fibers in de-inking plants. Purchasing can contribute to such design for reuse, recycling, and disassembly by suggesting alternative sources of supply and early supplier design involvement options.

The emphasis placed by firms on "environmentalism" has grown rapidly in the recent past. Most firms approach environmental issues defensively, in that managers are careful not to "violate the law" in considering their business decisions; however certain leading-edge firms like Hewlett Packard, Xerox, 3M and Daimler Benz are starting to compete on the basis of positive environmental reputation for their products and processes. The existing literature on environmental practices has increased exponentially and encompasses disciplines such as economics, operations management, law, organizational theory, and engineering. For the most part, this literature describes the motives for paying attention to environmental issues, leading-edge environmental practices, barriers for considering environmental issues, legal issues relating to the environment, and uniform standards for assessing environmental impact. To a lesser extent, the literature has started to address issues relating to integration of environmental objectives into strategic decisions. For example, the concept of design for environment (DFE), which involves the proactive assessment of environmental impact associated with the product being designed, has been adopted by several manufacturing firms. A much smaller body of literature has started to examine generic environmental strategies that firms pursue. In practice, many firms have found that incorporation of environmentalism can be costly. Other firms recognize the importance of considering environmental issues but lack the understanding of necessary processes to manage them.

IMPORTANCE

Today, purchasing managers are in a better position than they have ever been to knowledgeably modify procurement specifications and substitute more environmentally friendly materials, by using new software programs and reporting systems that provide them with environmental information on supply chain sourcing options [*Purchasing,* Feb. 16, 1996: 25; Kopicki et al., 1993). Clearly, the purchasing function's role can go far beyond merely reducing waste, by auditing the supply chain for life-cycle costs, design for disassembly and reuse opportunities, and supplier technology development programs.

Several studies have examined the extent to which firms are pursuing environmental practices and strategies. For example, Wheeler (1992) reported that 90 percent of the CEOs of firms studied projected that the environmental challenge was going to be one of the central issues of the next century. Similarly, Lent and Wells (1991) found that environmental management was a central part of corporate strategy in several *Fortune* 200 companies. The purchasing function has an increasingly important role in its contribution to a firm's environmental strategy. In a recent survey of purchasing executives, Min and Galle (1997) found that more than half the respondents indicated that their company had an environmental auditing program. Nevertheless, the role of the purchasing function in environmental strategies is a support role and in most firms does not extend to suppliers' operations. This was found in the Min and Galle study which reported that in only 31.9 percent of the firms that were surveyed was suppliers' environmental capability one of the criteria for ensuring suppliers' quality assurance.

In a recent research study sponsored by the Center for Advanced Purchasing Studies (CAPS) on the future directions and trends of purchasing and supply management (Carter and Narasimhan, 1996) environmentally sensitive purchasing was ranked fourth in terms of most significant trends affecting purchasing and supply management by European purchasing executives. In sharp contrast, North American purchasing executives did not consider this trend to be important. However, as is confirmed in a later study by Min and Galle, North American purchasing executives are beginning to realize the usefulness of incorporating environmental considerations in purchasing decisions. This change comes partly in response to the "environmentally conscious manufacturing" movement currently under way in several industries most notably in automotive, furniture, and other durable goods industries.

RESEARCH OBJECTIVES

As suggested in the above examples, procurement personnel can play a key role in environmental activities. Purchasing serves as a boundary spanning function within the supply chain (Day and Wensley, 1983; Leenders and Fearon, 1993; Webster, 1992; Williams et al., 1994). By being at the firm's boundary, purchasing is in an advantageous position to assess the inter-organizational environment for product and process change (Porter and van der Linde, 1995a). This knowledge enables managers to identify external trends and to respond by adopting suitable supply chain management strategies (McGuire et al., 1988). Despite the obvious importance of environmental issues, little research has been performed that examines the role of the purchasing function in managing the supply chain for environmental advantage.

This CAPS study was commissioned as a "theory development" study aimed at examining environmental issues of relevance to supply chain management. Environmental Supply Chain Management (ESCM) is an emerging field. Although there have been research studies on ESCM, few have attempted to examine strategic as well as methodological issues using in-depth, multiple case studies. The research objectives of this study are to:

- Briefly summarize the relevant literature relating to environmental practices.

- Describe which practices currently are being emphasized in a sample of leading edge firms in North America and Europe.

- Describe the supply chain management implications resulting from these practices.

- Describe in detail a select set of environmental management tools and practices.

- Develop a framework and a process by which environmental issues can be incorporated in supply chain management strategies.

- Propose pertinent issues for purchasing executives to consider in the future based on current and projected trends relating to environmentalism.

PARTICIPATING FIRMS

To investigate these research objectives, firms known to have made exemplary progress in implementing environmental strategies based on reports in the popular press and suggestions from industry sources were solicited for possible participation in this research project. The consenting firms from North America and Europe represent diverse industries such as pharmaceuticals, chemicals, automotive (including their first-tier suppliers), and domestic appliances. These firms serve as potential benchmarking partners for firms desirous of implementing environmental strategies successfully. The firms participating in this project are:

3M Corporation
Daimler Benz, AG
Dekra Umwelt GmbH
DENSO Manufacturing Michigan, Inc.
Eli Lilly
Grundfos
Hoechst AG
Honda of America Manufacturing
Novartis (formerly, Ciba-Geigy)
Novo Nordisk
Oscorna
Sidler GMBH and Co.
UZIN Georg Utz Gmbh & Co.
Whirlpool Corporation

RESEARCH METHODOLOGY

This research project explores the pervasive impact of environmental issues across the supply chain. As indicated previously, only firms known to have made substantial progress in implementing environmental strategies were invited to participate in the study. Care was taken to ensure sufficient diversity in terms of products, markets served, and industry type in the final sample of firms. Because the literature on environmental supply chain strategies is very limited, efforts relating to systematic theory building in this area are most amenable to case study research methodologies. The research process for theory building using case study data usually involves: defining the research objective, selecting the cases, designing survey instruments or interview protocols, collecting the data, analyzing the data, inferring research propositions, and relating the propositions to the literature and future practice. This methodology was adhered to in collecting case study data during field visits to participating firms.

In most cases, the initial contact person was from a single corporate department such as the environmental affairs or the purchasing department. The contact person always referred the researchers to other knowledgeable executives within the company. Functional backgrounds of these executives varied from senior purchasing managers to design and process engineers. The discussions followed a semi-structured format; most interviews followed a pattern of questions dealing with company background, drivers for environmentally sensitive management, environmental practices being emphasized by the firm, and implications of such practices for supply chain management. However, the discussion was not controlled by the researchers and respondents would typically divert from the general pattern to include supplier practices, global practices (i.e., comparisons across geographical regions), and technical details of innovative product and process design, which had an impact on environmental performance. This discussion was subsequently "funneled" into a discussion as to whether or not an emphasis on environmental practice was economically viable.

INFORMATION ANALYSIS

Following each interview, the field study notes were transcribed resulting in copious pages of raw case data. The general format of discussion questions (i.e., background, drivers, practices, and implications for supply chain management) served as a template for writing up the case study reports. Instead of using a coding mechanism to identify key concepts (as has been suggested by Miles and Huberman, 1984), this study used the uncoded raw data to identify suggestive environmental themes that underlie leading-edge practice. As such, this appeared to be a "better" method because its simplicity suited the exploratory nature of this study. If the concept identification method had been used, it would have been too broad and more difficult to identify a small set of concept categories or themes dealing with environmental supply chain management. Moreover, the primary objective of this research project was to discern the implications of ESCM for purchasing practice. Because the

ensuing themes were sufficiently broad, several matrices were constructed to cross-tabulate the themes and relate them to business strategy, manufacturing strategy, and purchasing practice. This cross-tabulation was helpful in the final stage of the research project pertaining to inference and implications for future purchasing practice.

This research report is organized into the following chapters:

1. Introduction
2. Literature Review
3. Case Studies
4. Generic Tools for Environmental Supply Chain Management
5. Cross-Case Analysis
6. Managerial Implications

CHAPTER 2: LITERATURE REVIEW •

Numerous case studies have broadly examined the importance of environmental issues (Porter and van der Linde, 1995a; Porter and van der Linde, 1995b; Dorfman et al., 1992). In addition, many studies have been performed that pertain to various aspects of supply chain management (Kopicki et al., 1993; Guiltinan and Nwokoye, 1975; Pohlen and Farris, 1992; Jahre, 1995; Stock, 1992). The logistics literature often focuses on the role of transportation managers in environmental endeavors such as recycling (Bronstad and Evans-Correia, 1992). The supply chain management literature, which frequently mentions environmental issues, is in its early stage, and as such tends to be exploratory in nature. Only recently has grounded research begun to emerge (Drumwright, 1994; Klassen and McLaughlin, 1993; Klassen and McLaughlin, 1996; Murphy et al., 1994; Murphy et al., 1995; Livingstone and Sparks, 1995). However, a relatively broad perspective that examines environmental purchasing activities simultaneously including substitution, reuse, recycling, and resource reduction has yet to emerge.

Overall, the review of the literature suggests that the current extent of knowledge concerning the role of purchasing managers in a firm's environmental endeavors is just beginning. An opportunity exists to expand upon previous research by developing and testing a theoretical framework that examines the factors that are driving and constraining environmental purchasing activities.

A firm's environmental purchasing activities are affected by a host of intra-organizational factors, including a sincere commitment to environmental issues, successfully implemented ethical standards, an adequate reward and incentive system, and the existence of "policy entrepreneurs" who make a strong commitment to and take personal responsibility for organizational adoption of an environmentally friendly philosophy (Gray and Guthrie, 1990; Winsemius and Guntram, 1992; Carter and Ellram, 1998).

The push for "environmentalism" is characterized through the development and refinement of three important themes: the application of total quality management (TQM) principles to environmental management, total quality environmental management (TQEM); the importance of considering environmental issues in manufacturing strategy, environmentally conscious manufacturing (ECM); and the utilization of environmentally sensitive manufacturing themes across the supply chain, environmental supply chain management (ESCM). These three themes are described under their respective headings.

TOTAL QUALITY ENVIRONMENTAL MANAGEMENT

The quality revolution, and in particular, the success of quality programs has prompted firms to apply these principles to the area of environmental management. These principles are collectively known as total quality environmental management (TQEM). Specifically, elements of TQM as suggested in the Malcolm Baldrige Award, customer focus, leadership, information and analysis, strategic planning, human resource development, quality assurance, and business results have been useful for implementation of total quality environmental management in companies such as Eastman Kodak Company and Great Lakes Industries (Wever and Vorhauer, 1993). In the latter company, the Baldrige TQM criteria served as a facilitating measurement tool for excellence in environmental management. For example, under the category of information and analysis, basic information relating to compliance, pollution prevention, and sustainability must be collected and analyzed. Similarly, under the category of business results, identification of appropriate measures for capturing performance on compliance, waste reduction, and satisfaction of customers' need for "greener" products is important.

By learning from the TQM movement, many companies are examining ways to integrate environmental performance into the management and operation of their core business processes (Haines, 1993). For example, Xerox instituted reuse of packaging and pallets based on a standardized design that resulted in a reduction of 10,000 tons of waste and savings of $15 million annually. AT&T redesigned its circuit-board cleaning process that involved an elimination of the use of chemicals, which resulted in annual savings of $3 million. Reynolds Metals replaced solvent-based ink with water-based inks in packaging plants that lowered the emission rate by 65 percent and saved the company $30 million in production equipment. Thus, the application of TQM principles, such as waste reduction, reuse, and efficient design of products and processes, has facilitated the successful incorporation of environmental management into the mainstream of business operations.

ENVIRONMENTALLY CONSCIOUS MANUFACTURING

In a recent survey, Wheeler (1992) reported that 90 percent of the CEOs who were surveyed projected that the environmental challenge was sure to be one of the central issues of the next century. Similarly, Lent and Wells (1991) found that environmental management was a central part of corporate strategy in several *Fortune* 200 companies. environmentally conscious manufacturing (ECM) involves the planning, development, and implementation of manufacturing processes and technology that minimize or eliminate hazardous waste, reduce scrap, are operationally safer, and products that are recyclable, or can be remanufactured or reused (Weissman and Sekutowski, 1991). This definition suggests that the proactive consideration of environmental issues in product and process design can be a source of competitive advantage. Proactive product-related issues include designing for remanufacturability, recyclability, and reusability. Examples of process-related issues include design and development of life-cycle analysis standards, waste monitoring systems, and disassembly for manufacturing processes.

ENVIRONMENTAL SUPPLY CHAIN MANAGEMENT

Supply chain integration and management has recently received a great deal of attention from researchers and practitioners alike. Xerox, Hewlett Packard, AlliedSignal, and Siemens are examples of firms that have attempted to operationalize supply chain integration with varying degrees of success in their respective industries (Leenders, Nollet, and Ellram, 1994). Research on supply chain management has focussed mainly on individual functions such as purchasing, manufacturing, and logistics (Cavinato, 1992; Scott and Westbrook, 1991; and Turner, 1993). Studies that have examined the use of environmentally sensitive manufacturing practices across the supply chain (i.e., across functional and organizational boundaries) are relatively rare. For example, Johannson (1994) reports the example of Consumer Glass, a Canadian ceramic manufacturer that uses a new form of supply chain management in a recursive situation when the customer becomes a supplier in the reverse logistics process. The reverse process involves recycled glass as an input to generate cullet that is the raw material in the buyer's manufacturing process. So the traditional supply chain cycle changes in form from supplier-buyer-customer to supplier-buyer-consumer-buyer. This new notion introduces the idea of "detracted" value as opposed to added value in the supply chain. For example, if in the value chain one of the channel partners adds liability to the value-added in the form of less-environmentally conscious input, then this partner is defined as having detracted value in the supply chain. Although current discussions in the supply chain management literature and in practice are focused on customer value creation, future debate and discussion will place equal emphasis on "detracted value" environmental supply chain management gains wider acceptance.

ESCM will increase in importance as the push to create high customer value through cost reduction becomes well entrenched.

REASONS FOR ADOPTING TQEM, ECM, AND ESCM

There are both external and internal reasons for adopting environmental conscious strategies in business operations. The internal reasons are due to a proactive stance toward the use of environmental strategies as a source of competitive advantage. The external reason is mainly in response to regulation from governmental agencies and product and environmental liabilities.

Strategic Drivers

Corporations have been confronted recently with a number of global environmental challenges such as global warming, acid rain, depletion of natural resources, waste management, green consumerism, and pollution prevention. This has prompted a higher level of environmental awareness throughout organizations, including the need to integrate core environmental operating principles in making effective business decisions. For example, Avery Dennison uses the core elements of ISO 14001 that include an environmental stewardship policy, specific environmental operating principles, environmental accountability for proper operations, and an environmental management system as a basis for integrating core environmental operating principles in making effective business decisions (Fear, 1995). The environmental management system used by this company is similar to the Global Environmental Management Initiative's (GEMI) environmental self-assessment tool.

It has been argued that firms that do not recognize the implications of environmental problems on business processes will not realize long-term success in the competitive marketplace (Gupta, 1995). Various environmental management practices provide opportunities to strengthen a firm's distinctive competence in terms of operational objectives such as highest quality, lowest cost, best dependability, and greatest flexibility. Using experiences of a few firms, researchers recently have proposed process models that provide links between environmental management, operations strategy, and corporate strategy (Gupta, 1995; Sarkis,1995; Wu and Dunn, 1995; Klassen,1993). For example, Klassen (1993) proposed a framework for integrating environmental issues into manufacturing that recognized the bidirectional interaction among the marketplace, government agencies, and manufacturing. In sum, the adoption and diffusion of process models reiterate the growing importance accorded to integration of environmental issues in strategic plans.

Regulations

Government regulations also play a key role in influencing environmentally sensitive business operations. For example, the Environmental Protection Agency (EPA) formulates guidelines on acquisition of environmentally preferable products and services that are applicable to federal procurement of all kinds of consumer and commercial products and services (Bryson and Donohue, 1996). The guidance involves the following principles of making procurement decisions:

Principle 1: *Early consideration of environmental preference in the acquisition process that aims at eliminating or reducing potential risks to human health and the environment.*

This principle directs the purchaser to examine not only the environmental efficiency of the end-use product being purchased, but also the manufacturing process that produces the product. For example, the principle would not be satisfied by examining whether a halogenated solvent cleaner is better or worse for the environment than an aqueous-based cleaner. Rather, it requires an examination of whether the cleaning/degreasing step can be eliminated altogether without affecting the overall performance of the product or system. Clearly, this has greater applicability where a customized purchase or product is involved, and where substantial design period in which to evaluate such issues is given.

Principle 2: *Recognizing that a product's or service's environmental preference is a function of multiple attributes.*

This principle specifies the need to identify and understand the multiple environmental attributes of any given product or service. While single environmental performance characteristics such as energy efficiency or recycled content are more easily defined, measured, and understood, it is possible to overlook other important environmental impacts of the product or service. This principle involves identifying four important attributes that can be used to determine environmentally preferable products or services. These are natural resources use, human health and ecological stressors, positive attributes, and hazard factors associated with the product. These attributes are used to provide a composite index of environmental preference.

In the natural resources attribute, a range of impacts such as the affect on the ecosystem (endangered species, wetlands loss, fragile ecosystem etc.), energy consumption, water consumption, and non-renewable resource consumption is used. Ten separate stressors are listed under the human health and ecological stressor characteristic, including bio-accumulative pollutants, ozone-depleting chemicals, global-warming gases, chemical releases, ambient air releases, indoor environmental

release, conventional pollutants released to water, hazardous waste, non-hazardous solid waste, and a catch-all category for all other stressors. Positive attributes include recycled content, product disassembly potential, durability, and reusability, which relate to reusing or extending the life of the product so as to minimize the use of additional resources. Hazard factors associated with the product include human health hazards such as acute toxicity, carcinogenicity, developmental/reproductive toxicity, immunotoxicity, irritancy, and sensitization. Other hazards include ecological hazards (aquatic, avian, and terrestrial species toxicity) and product safety hazards (corrosivity, flammability, and reactivity).

Principle 3: *Environmental preference should consider the scale (global vs. local) and temporal reversibility aspects of the impact.*

This principle recognizes that effects may not be easily compared. For example, the impact of increased energy requirements for one product may be more tolerable than the water pollutants associated with the use of another product. Similarly, with respect to ecological risks, a matrix that associates ecological recovery time (reversibility of damages) against geographical scale of the risk can be used to decide environmental preference. Ecological recovery time is measured in years, decades, or centuries, and geographical scale is measured on a nominal scale of local/regional, national, and global.

Principle 4: *Product attribute claims must be carefully examined.*

This principle addresses the need to ensure accuracy of environmental performance information. Two general sources of information are typically used: manufacturer information and certification programs awarded by third-party environmental agencies. Examples of manufacturer information include information provided on product labels and in advertisements. Third-party certification programs award seals of approval or verifies manufacturer-specific claims.

Stakeholder Management

Besides regulation, the opportunity to serve the environmental interests of key stakeholders such as environmental groups, regulatory authorities, and corporate neighbors is serving as a stimulus for environmentally sensitive operations. For example, in Novo Nordisk the stakeholder management process starts with the identification of key stakeholder groups that include the media, employees, investors, insurance companies, customers and suppliers, local authorities, universities, and the European Union (EU). Next the order of priority among these groups is determined. An interaction process wherein formal and informal dialogues are started with an intention to understand the needs of the different stakeholder groups follows this. The formal communication process takes place through dissemination of environmental progress reports among the key stakeholder groups, journalist briefings, customer workshops, and technical briefings for local authorities. The informal dialogue process is done through site visits to the company, roundtables for local and international environmental groups, and neighbor meetings at the plants. Finally, the views of the different stakeholder groups are considered in formulating environmental strategies.

Globalization Of Markets

Globalization of markets for most finished products has also contributed to environmental sensitivity. Traditionally, nations were competitive if their companies had access to the lowest cost inputs — capital, labor, energy, and raw materials (Porter and van der Linde, 1995). Therefore, in industries that rely on natural resources, competitive companies and nations were those with abundant local supplies. Because technology changed slowly, a comparative advantage in inputs led to competitive success. In today's competitive environment, the notion of comparative advantage is obsolete. Global sourcing and rapid diffusion of technology can offset disadvantages in the cost of inputs. Therefore, it is the productive use of scarce resources that can lead to competitive advantages. For example, companies that pursue resource-wasting methods or forego environmental standards are likely to lose competitiveness in the global economy.

ENVIRONMENTAL TOOLS AND TECHNIQUES

Before turning to specific tools, it is important to point out one common approach to environmental strategy, the proactive strategy. Companies such as AT&T have changed their focus on environmental policies from compliance to pollution prevention (Thompson and Rauck, 1993). The company is committed to aggressive environmental and safety goals beyond those required by federal and state laws and regulations. Part of the strategy for pollution prevention involves the deployment of an integrated program that includes design for the environment, green manufacturing, and a comprehensive effort to reduce existing waste in production. Developing proactive environmental strategies involves defining target customers, measuring customer expectations, analyzing results, developing responsive programs and measuring the results of program implementation (Craig, 1992). For example, Apple Computer defines its customers as people who use or buy computers, people who buy stock, Apple employees, and Apple's extended family of neighbors and friends. Apple measures customer expectations and demands by tracking direct inquiries regarding the Apple's environmental effort, and by gathering indirect information from regulators, competitors, the press, and the environmental community. Honda of America follows a similar environmental strategy development process.

The ISO 14000 Certification

In the environmental arena, the effort to establish uniform standards for evaluating environmental performance has been evolving for years. Statute and regulation establish many of these standards. Other standards or assessment tools have also been proposed. For example, Apsan (1995) proposed an ISO 14000 scorecard called Environmental Performance Evaluation (EPE). EPE is proposed as an effective TQM tool for establishing a road map for continuous improvement and a model for understanding analytical perspectives or evaluation areas within the environmental management arena. 3M instituted a global environmental management system that not only functions to comply with environmental regulations, but also helps in preparation of meeting the requirements of international standards, such as ISO 14000 (Cysewski and Howell, 1995).

Integrated Environmental Audit

Environmental protection is a key issue for a publicly held company, and most companies have organizational structures that include a corporate-level environmental management function. In a recent survey, it was reported that audits of the environmental management function were conducted by more than 90 percent of the responding companies, with the most common type of audit being those related to regulatory compliance (Campbell and Byington, 1995). The scope of the environmental auditing programs in many of the companies surveyed included audits of pollution prevention and waste minimization programs, compliance with company environmental policies, and evaluation of environmental practices of firms that were candidates for acquisition. Most companies reported that the greatest benefits of environmental auditing were related to compliance and avoidance of regulatory action. Environmental audit programs have also helped companies make significant improvements in environmental performance by using TQM principles in developing corrective actions and evaluating company performance (Hedstrom and Voeller, 1993). For example, in Novo Nordisk, all suppliers and contractors are audited to ensure that the goods and services they provide are environmentally sound. Key suppliers are issued a 30-page questionnaire asking for documentation of the suppliers' environmental management systems, environmental impacts, and product composition.

Life-Cycle Analysis/Assessment

Life-cycle assessment (LCA) is an analytical tool that evaluates the environmental consequences of a product, process, or activity across its entire life cycle

(Gloria et al., 1995). LCA is used internationally by government and industry to obtain a comprehensive perspective of the interactions between an activity and the environment, and LCA provides a method to systematically identify opportunities for improvement. External forces such as eco-labels and the recent development of the ISO 14000 standards drive the use of LCA. Huang and Hunkeler (1995), in a mail survey of 175 U.S. corporations from the *Fortune* 500 list, found that more than half the 56 respondents were using life-cycle concepts for environmental assessments. Marketing and cost issues were stated as the primary motivation factors for implementing life-cycle analysis. The survey also reported that life-cycle thinking was not adequately integrated throughout corporate organizations, and was more prevalent within the environmental affairs department.

A survey of 26 large industrial companies revealed that firms, especially in the electronics and consumer products sectors, are now using, developing, or considering the use of life-cycle frameworks (Sullivan and Ehrenfeld, 1992). Product design and development and other technical departments are highly involved in life-cycle work, but finance, accounting, and legal departments are absent from life-cycle work at almost all firms. The primary motivation for life-cycle assessment was found to be the desire to capitalize on strategic and market opportunities and to gather information on environmental concerns of customers. In the automotive industry, the U.S. Council for Automotive Research, a partnership of the Big Three United States automobile manufacturers, has recommended that the Big Three firms and their suppliers use life-cycle assessment for benchmarking environmental performance of vehicles; evaluating recycling options; assessing environmentally friendly material choices in design stage; assessing the environmental performance of their suppliers; and improving business processes (Bari, 1995).

Another variation of life-cycle cost analysis is life-cycle cost management (LCCM), which is a structured process for making decisions based on the true cost of the products and processes rather than on purchase price alone or on other partial life-cycle costs (Gess and Cohan, 1994). Several utility companies have used LCCM to evaluate a range of product substitution and process improvement decisions and to implement cost-saving actions. LCCM has helped utilities save millions of dollars by considering the true costs of the materials, products, and processes they use.

At the same time, the cost of conducting comprehensive LCA exercises can be cost prohibitive because certain stages of the LCA methodology (for example, impact and improvement assessment) are not well developed. To address this problem, companies such as GKN in the United Kingdom have combined LCA with another tool, design for the environment (DFE), to provide a mechanism for tracking real improvements in environmental efficiency.

Design For Environment (DFE)

The increasing market demand for green products underscores the critical importance of a systematic approach to the design of products and processes used to build, ship, support, and recover products (Paton, 1993). For example, leading companies are using *design for environment* (DFE) practices by addressing environmental issues in the initial design process; this results in the most cost-effective means for minimizing negative environmental impacts (Fiksel, 1993). Developing an effective DFE capability involves evaluating environmental quality in objective, measurable terms to facilitate goal setting, monitoring, and continuous improvement in the design of products and processes. In particular, a life-cycle view of environmental performance helps in the tracking of environmental quality.

Several companies, including AT&T, General Electric, IBM, Procter & Gamble, Whirlpool, and Xerox, are considering environmental compatibility while designing new products through the use of a variety of strategies such as design for environment (DFE) that aim to design environmental improvements into each stage of a product's life cycle (Oakley, 1993). Companies can use life-cycle analysis to quantify the environmental impacts and tradeoffs of their products at each stage. The most important component of this new design paradigm is that all people involved in the product realization process work together as an integrated team. For example, AT&T has developed the term Design for "X" (DFX), where "X" represents a number of downstream product criteria. In DFX, all personnel involved in a new product's development are part of a multifunctional, integrated team.

Reverse Logistics

Reengineering the structure and management of the supply chain through reverse logistics has been proposed as a method for reducing or eliminating the generation of waste in the supply chain (Giuntini, 1996). In reverse logistics, the ownership and liability of impaired material resources are transferred from the customer back to the supplier. There is an implicit assumption that the supplier must redesign its products and processes to eliminate or minimize waste. Failure to eliminate or minimize waste while designing products results in higher costs associated with managing impaired material resources. To support reverse logistics, an organization must develop a vastly expanded infrastructure and management system that creates new organizational decision-making drivers.

Company-Specific Methods

Apart from the generic environmental tools described previously, several companies have developed company-specific environmental methods and tools. One of the methods companies have used to improve environmental performance is the measuring of safety performance. Safety performance has a direct effect on employees' productivity and quality of work life, and on company profits and image in the community. Enormous human and financial losses can result from poor safety performance, and all such losses are preventable. To prevent these potential losses, safety performance must be continually improved across all levels of the organization. For example, Kodak uses a performance management tool called safety performance indexing to help improve environmental and occupational health performance throughout the company (Kiser and Esler, 1995).

Wise (1995) reports the case of Ciba-Geigy, a specialty chemical and pharmaceutical company, that used teams to manage more than 100 waste remediation sites in 38 states. The potential cost exceeded $500 million. The sites varied in their scope and technical complexity. Four regional remediation teams with similar reporting structure and a sense of ownership helped manage the complex remediation sites.

AT&T uses TQM methodologies to turn its environmental focus from end-of-pipe waste management to proactive and preventive TQEM as evidenced by the many products and services that have received the ISO 9000 certification and awards such as the Malcolm Baldrige Award and the Deming Prize for Quality (Dambach and Allenby, 1995). Similarly, at Boeing, the environmental assessment monitoring program was revised to incorporate TQM themes such as identification of corrective actions, promoting ongoing communication between the safety, health, and environmental affairs unit and sites on resolving compliance issues, and checking for compliance with standards using quality control techniques (Rodenhurst, and Spens, 1993). The revised process has resulted in an 86-percent reduction in time required to finalize the environmental assessment report and action plans.

Although internal TQEM efforts do improve the environmental impact of a firm's operations, most firms remain focused on the traditional bottom-line objective of increasing throughput and velocity. For these reasons, most firms implementing TQEM miss many opportunities to improve environmental performance through asset recovery, resource sharing, and reuse. Inter-firm teaming for environmental advantage, which is defined as "TQEM alliancing," initiates a cyclical approach to environmental performance improvement (O'Dea and Pratt, 1995). "TQEM *alliancing*" forges strategic relationships among firms that can leverage each other's environmen-

tal strengths. It allows firms to take their environmental improvement initiatives beyond regulatory compliance and into proactivity, beyond pollution control to total pollution avoidance, and beyond profitability for a quantitative as well as qualitative bottom line, by integrating external as well as internal functions across different business domains.

In today's world, most corporations have multimillion dollar environmental programs, and manufacturing sites have environmental departments with budgets in the $100,000 range (Iannuzzi, 1995). Many environmental managers have been asked to reduce budgets in a regulatory marketplace that keeps adding requirements at a hectic pace. Reengineering of environmental processes has been proposed as a method of achieving efficiencies in resource utilization and at the same time increasing customer service levels (Iannuzzi, 1995).

Successful implementation of environmental management information systems (EMIS) has become essential to the success of total quality environmental management (TQEM) programs (FitzGerald, 1994). Effective EMIS programs are effective in developing metrics, models, and tools that are based on business processes rather than regulatory edicts. FitzGerald (1994) states that the use of EMIS programs has become extremely popular in electric power companies.

Firms have also used environmental performance measurement as a means to upgrade environmental management systems (Miakisz, 1994). At Niagara Mohawk Power Corporation (NMPC), an environmental performance index (EPI) was developed. It utilizes a weight and rating scheme to reflect environmental performance in three categories: emissions-wastes, regulatory compliance, and environmental enhancements. Performance goals are established for future periods, and actual performance data are collected and compared to projections. Calculating each parameter contained in the emissions-waste category and adjusting annual reductions or increases in pollutants for each year relative to the benchmark forms the EPI. A composite score is determined at the end of each calendar year. Similarly, the experience of Ontario Hydro, Canada's largest public utility, points to the fact that both the tracking and quantification of environmental efforts enable companies to become leaders on environmental issues (Wolfe and Howes, 1993). In measuring performance, three issues should be considered: identifying performance indicators, the challenge of measurement, and communicating and using the data.

Another popular environmental performance measurement scheme is called Global Environment Management Initiative's (GEMI) environmental self-assessment procedure (ESAP) (Morton, 1994). The ESAP reflects a company's perceived rating of environmental performance that can be different from actual performance, depending on the objectivity exercised and the level of compliance assurance information available. The ESAP allows companies to assess their environmental performance against the International Chamber of Commerce's Business Charter for Sustainable Development. ESAP scoring is based on a scale of 0 to 4, with a score of one characterized by a general goal to achieve substantial regulatory compliance. A score of 4 represents the best score and is characterized by application of proactive leadership techniques and practices, including total quality management principles. The ESAP format is designed to rate the effectiveness and implementation of elements that comprise each characteristic of environmental management systems.

IMPLICATIONS FOR ENVIRONMENTAL SUPPLY CHAIN MANAGEMENT

The literature review hypothesizes a set of the internal and external drivers of environmental purchasing activities. Some research has provided a multi-variate empirical examination of the inter-firm change forces to identify which of these factors are key driver(s) of environmental purchasing activities (Carter, 1996); however, more can be done to identify the primary inter-organizational drivers of environmental purchasing that can help managers to allocate limited resources toward management of those parts of the supply chain that are having the greatest impact on a firm's environmental effectiveness.

The literature review also suggests that upstream members of a supply chain can limit the effectiveness of environmental purchasing activities through uncertainty of the availability of resources, poor quality of environmentally efficient inputs, and insufficient coordination with suppliers of these inputs.

An understanding of the inter-organizational supply chain environment enables managers to identify external trends and to respond by adopting suitable strategies (McGuire et al., 1988). Day and Wensley (1983) and Webster (1992) note that marketing is a boundary-spanning function within each firm that is in an advantageous position to assess the inter-organizational environment. Industrial marketing and purchasing are on opposite ends of the same dyadic relationship, and this places the purchasing function in an advantageous position to assess a firm's supply chain competencies. The reviewed literature suggests that government regulation, a firm's customers, suppliers, and competitors (its supply chain) are affecting environmental purchasing activities (Carter and Ellram, 1998).

The three themes of total quality environmental management (TQEM), environmentally conscious manufacturing (ECM), and environmental supply chain management (ESCM) have implications for green supply chain management. For example, incorporation of environmental issues in sourcing decisions is beginning to emerge. Jamison (1996) reports a case study of a retailing company that instituted an environmentally conscious purchasing program. This program included a supplier environmental audit with the objective of monitoring the environmental performance of suppliers. Communication with suppliers and incentives for superior environmental performance were found to be the two key elements of successful supplier management in achieving environmental goals. Suppliers were assessed against environmental criteria that were aimed at preventing the generation of waste at the earliest opportunity. A formal assessment process called QUEST was used to evaluate suppliers against 10 criteria, five of which were related to quality and five to environmental issues. The aim of QUEST was to assess the quality, safety and treatment of a product before it was manufactured, and thus reduce the problem of perpetual "fire fighting." Also, in a recent survey of purchasing executives belonging to the National Association of Purchasing Management (NAPM), environmental factors were identified as one of the factors influencing future supplier selection decisions. Similarly, environmental purchasing has an influence on decisions relating to packaging, waste reduction, and waste elimination.

Despite the growing literature base in environmental management, very few studies have examined environmental supply chain issues in sufficient detail. Even within this literature, more attention is paid to issues relating to the different drivers of environmentalism and environmental tools and methodologies, and relatively less attention is paid to strategies or how environmental issues are successfully incorporated into corporate strategy development and decision making. Generic environmental strategies and "how-to" frameworks for deploying environmental strategies are non-existent.

This research study is geared toward developing future-oriented frameworks of successful incorporation of environmental issues in the supply chain. The detailed case studies are described in the next chapter, and following the case studies is a description of some key environmental tools and methods used in the case studies. In the subsequent chapters, a detailed content analysis of the cases is undertaken and the ensuing propositions are summarized. In the final chapter, implications of environmental issues on supply chain management are offered.

CHAPTER 3: CASE STUDIES •

3M CORPORATION

COMPANY BACKGROUND

Minnesota Mining and Manufacturing (3M) is a diversified company with operations in three main sectors: Industrial and Consumer Products; Information, Imaging, and Electronics Products; and Life Sciences Products. 3M's products include tape, fax machines, and film. Fifty percent of its sales are from overseas operations, and the company continues to expand outside the United States, particularly in the Pacific Rim. The company's vision is to be not only the most innovative enterprise in all activities such as purchasing and human resource management but also to be the preferred supplier for its customers. 3M's success has traditionally come from producing innovative solutions to customers' problems. For example, products such as Wetordry Sandpaper, Post-it Notes and Scotchgard Fabric Protectors have changed the way consumers use products.

3M serves an extraordinarily diverse group of 12 markets — automotive, communication arts, construction/maintenance, consumer products, electronics/electrical, healthcare, industrial products, office products, pharmaceuticals, safety and security, telecommunications, and transportation; catering to a wide variety of industrial and consumer durable types of customers. It manufactures or sells more than 50,000 products in categories such as abrasives/minerals, adhesives, advanced materials, electrical/ telecommunications, health science, non-woven, optics, and precision coating. Almost all these products are the result of combining 3M's core technologies in ways that solve customers' problems. These technologies, and the imaginative application of them, have contributed to the company's competitive advantage. Some technology, like abrasives and adhesives, are established innovations that trace as far back as 1925 (masking tape); 1930 (cellophane tape); 1948 (adhesive surgical drapes); and 1953 (Scotch-Weld Structural Adhesives). More recent innovations include the now famous Post-it Notes▣, which were introduced in 1980.

OPERATING HIGHLIGHTS

In 1996, the company's sales totaled $14.2 billion, an increase of about 9 percent in local currencies and 5.8 percent in U.S. dollars. International sales were $7.6 billion, representing 53 percent of total sales. During the last three years the company's sales have grown nearly 9

percent a year, income from continuing operations has increased by more than 10 percent a year, and earnings per share from continuing operations have grown 11.6 percent a year.

The company continues to hold leading positions in certain market segments. For example, the Industrial and Consumer Sector is the world's largest supplier of tapes, producing more than 900 varieties. This sector is also a leader in coated abrasives, specialty chemicals, repositionable notes, home cleaning sponges and pads, and electronic circuits. The Life Sciences Sector is a global leader in reflective materials for transportation safety, respirators for worker safety, closures for disposable diapers, and high-quality indoor and outdoor graphics. This sector also holds leading positions in medical and surgical supplies, drug delivery systems, and dental products.

The company's success in growth can be attributed to three initiatives: supply chain excellence, pacing plus, and earning customer loyalty. In 3M there is a deliberate focus on all business systems with a view of attaining supply chain excellence. In the pacing plus initiative, the company looks at new products that have a significant income potential and then introduces the product to the market as quickly as possible. Under customer loyalty, the focus is working with customers and meeting their needs. As part of building strong customer relationships, 3M helps solve the environmental-related problems in their customer's operations.

The company's corporate values include a commitment to:

- satisfying customers with superior quality and value
- providing investors with an attractive return through sustained, high-quality growth
- respecting the social and physical environment around them
- being a company that employees are proud to be a part of

These values permeate the environmental initiatives of the company. For example, the CEO has an annual environmental leadership award program for employees.

ENVIRONMENTAL POSTURE OF THE COMPANY

Brief History of Environmental Management

In 3M, the emphasis on environmental issues started as early as 1961. Over a period of three decades, the company has made significant progress in environmental issues to serve as a benchmark for companies seeking to become superior performers on environmental issues. A brief history of environmental management in the company is summarized as follows:

- 1961—3M Water and Sanitary Engineering Department created.
- 1969—Starts program to stop landfilling liquid solvents.
- 1970—Environmental Engineering and Pollution Control (EE&PC) Organization formed; Product environmental assessments begin.
- 1973—Energy Management Department formed.
- 1975—Pollution Prevention Pays (3P) program initiated to stop pollution at source; Environmental policy adopted.
- 1976—3M Center wastepaper recycling program begins.
- 1980—PCB (polychlorinated biphenyls) phase-out program launched.
- 1981—Environmental audits of U.S. plants begin.
- 1987—Corporate Safety, Health and Environmental Committee established.
- 1988—CFC (chlorofluorocarbons) phaseout policy adopted.
- 1989—Year 2000 goals set to reduce all releases to air, water and land by 50 percent; Corporate Product Responsibility Group formed.
- 1990—Environmental marketing claims policy announced; Challenge'95 creates ambitious waste and energy reduction goals.
- 1991—Chairman's Environmental Leadership Award program launched.
- 1993—Goal of 70 percent reduction in 3M worldwide air emissions achieved.

Drivers for Environmental Consciousness

Within the company, an early emphasis on building a reputation for environmental excellence, especially among its customer base, was one of the key drivers for the company. Practices such as formulating a corporate environmental policy, forming a new environmental department, and launching more than 4,100 environment-related projects in the past 20 years are suggestive of environmental consciousness. A request made by the American Furniture Manufacturer's Association (AFMA) to serve as a potential benchmark on how to formulate and implement sound environmental policies for the company's major customer group, the furniture industry, was an important driver. 3M is a major supplier of coatings and sandpaper for the furniture industry. The company responded by creating a team that included members from AFMA to create a document that detailed environmental guidelines for the various product models manufactured and distributed by the firms. In another customer-oriented project, 3M teamed with AKZO Nobel (not a competitor) to create a strategic alliance called Radian. As part of this alliance, the company dedicated a project costing $120,000 to improve the environmentally conscious image of 3M among its customer base. In addition to learning credibility among its customers, the company also helped to speed up the permit-granting process administered by EPA, which helped in reducing overall cycle time. These examples suggest that firms whose environmental image is negative may lose competitive advantages even if the products sold by these companies have environmental benefits. On the other hand, as in the case of 3M, a strong environmental image and reputation can be leveraged to obtain competitive advantage for its products.

The company is also an early signatory to the ICC Charter for Sustainable Development. Participation in this important consortium shaped several environmental practices in the company. For example, the company integrates its environmental goals (called Year 2000 goals) with its long-term business objectives. The desire to standardize environmental operations on a global scale is also an important reason for an increasing emphasis on environmental consciousness.

3M'S ENVIRONMENTAL PRACTICES

Life-Cycle Management (LCM)

To pursue the objectives laid out in its environmental policy, several environmental practices are emphasized. For example, the company uses a life-cycle management (LCM) process to reduce the environmental impact of products at all stages from development to disposal. The significant progress made in the area of products and processes has been achieved mainly through the use of life-cycle assessment techniques. At each stage of the product life cycle from development through manufacturing, use, and disposal, the environmental, safety, and health impact of the product is assessed. The Corporate Product Responsibility Group was created in 1990 to promote life-cycle review, and provide training and technical help. Product responsibility coordinators in each business unit encourage and support life-cycle review at the technical level. In addition, each business unit has an executive to champion the process.

The primary motive behind developing a life-cycle management process was to manage the company's growing product base. The company has approximately 5,000 products and about 400 new products are introduced each year. The life-cycle model is a tool that assists business units in developing products with an optimum balance of performance, cost, and environmental, health, and safety (EHS) characteristics. The 3M life-cycle analysis (LCA) Process is shown in Figure 1 and the LCM process flow chart is shown in Figure 2. A team usually manages the LCA process. In each phase of the product life cycle, the team identifies problems relating to environment, health, and safety. For each problem, solution options are developed. Each solution is evaluated for its problem elimination benefits, as well as any new problems that may arise from the solution. The overarching objective of this problem identification-solution option exercise is to develop products that meet customer expectations, are highly competitive, and can be manufactured, distributed, used, and disposed of safely.

Representative activities and questions of interest in each of the four categories are now described. Under *"process,"* formal review of the manufacturing processes is undertaken to identify environmental, health and safety issues. For example, representative questions of interest are "What are the air, water and waste emissions from the process?" and "What are the hazardous wastes and possible employee exposures?" Another key activity is to identify and communicate environment-related risks for suppliers and contract manufacturers. Representative questions are "Which environment-related risks are the same for 3M's suppliers as they are for 3M's customers?" and "What are the opportunities to reduce these risks?"

Under *"distribution,"* review of the handling and transportation processes is undertaken to identify environmental, health and safety issues. For example, representative questions of interest are "Does the product require any special handling during its transportation to preserve its integrity?" and "Is the distributor qualified to provide safety-related communications and instructions to end customers?"

Under *"use,"* typical activities are to identify conditions under which customers use 3M's products. Representative issues of interest are assessing customer needs for training and education regarding safe and effective use and disposal of the product. Another issue may be to possibly restrict product sales to customers and markets based on the ability and willingness to use 3M's products safely.

Finally, under *"disposition,"* typical activities include considering the environmental hierarchy (of source reduction, reuse, recycle, and safe disposal) to reduce the environmental impact of product and packaging. For example, representative questions of interest are "Can the product be reformed into other products for different uses?" and "Should the company consider customer return of product/packaging waste?"

Another key consideration in the LCM process is the so-called "3P" elements of products, processes, and people (see Another Kind of "3P" in Figure 3). Each of these elements must be connected in the life-cycle management process. The larger the overlap among these three elements, the more the company progresses toward "sustainability." In 3M, sustainability is a corporate imperative. Currently, the company has reached the stage of homogeneous synergy among products, people, and processes.

Figure 4 presents an ideal product life-cycle model describing the four key processes of materials acquisition, manufacture, customer use, and recovery as the value chain in which there are "zero levels" of environmental impact. However, in reality there are several potential sources of harmful environmental effects (see Figure 5). For example, in the link between manufacturing and the customer, process-related losses, exposure to the "elements" and inadequate control systems may have a harmful environmental impact. Similarly, in the link between customer use and recovery, the workplace environment may be a contributing factor to poor environmental performance. For example, lack of proper training or safety guidelines may be the cause of poor workplace environment. Also, in the link between recovery and materials acquisition, inefficient transfers may mar the reuse process.

The potential problem areas identified in Figure 5 are really opportunities for improving the environmental performance through the LCM process (see Figure 6). For example, one possible source of eliminating or reducing the process losses and exposures phenomenon is to use materials and manufacturing processes that have low environmental impact. Similarly, the problems associated with the workplace environment can be mitigated through the proper identification and management of safety hazards.

SUPPLIER'S ENVIRONMENTAL CAPABILITY

The company conducts an environmental audit of every supplier who supplies direct material, develops an Environmental Management System structured to resemble ISO 14000 certification, and uses "gap analysis" for each element in the environmental management system.

ENVIRONMENTAL AUDITING

The in-house environmental audit program was started as early as in 1975 and much of it remains unchanged. The U.S. Environmental Compliance Audit Program in 3M was established in 1981. Its objectives are to:

FIGURE 1
3M LIFE-CYCLE ANALYSIS PROCESS

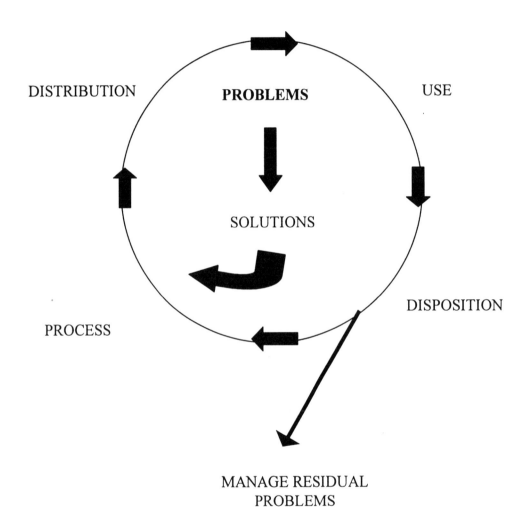

Source: 3M Corporation

FIGURE 2
LCM PROCESS FLOW CHART

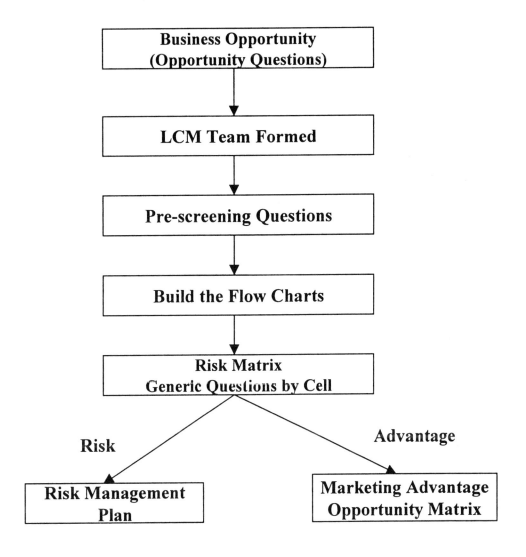

Source: 3M Corporation

FIGURE 3
ANOTHER KIND OF "3P"

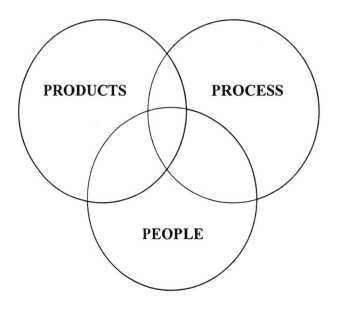

Source: 3M Corporation

FIGURE 4
3M PRODUCT LIFE-CYCLE - IDEAL

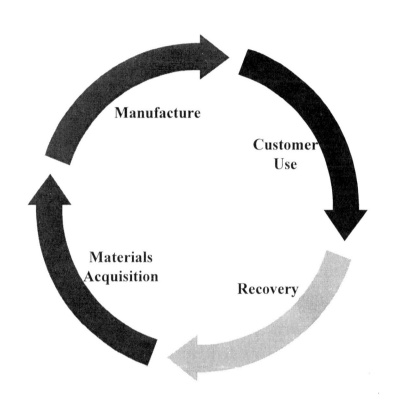

Source: 3M Corporation

FIGURE 5
3M PRODUCT LIFE-CYCLE - REALITY

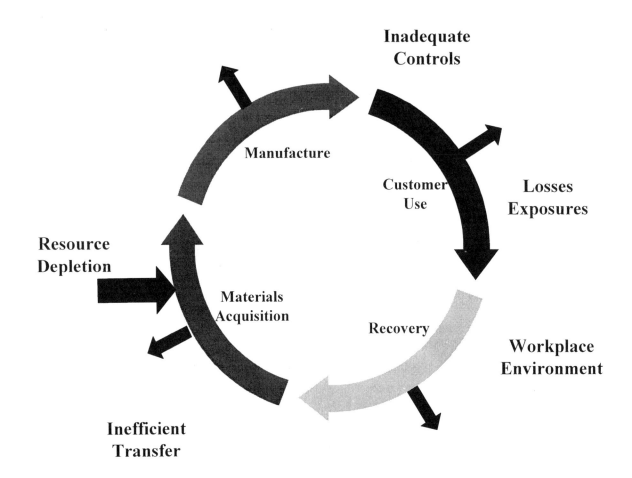

Source: 3M Corporation

FIGURE 6
3M LIFE-CYCLE MANAGEMENT - OPPORTUNITY

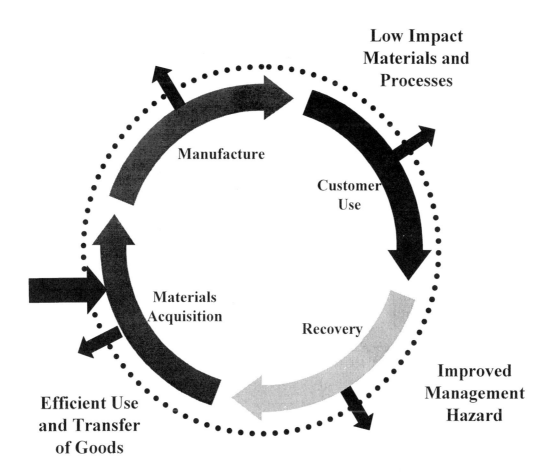

Source: 3M Corporation

- measure and ensure that procedures, practices and program comply with environmental regulations and 3M corporate policies
- identify potential environmental issues
- manage beyond compliance

The program is managed by an audit supervisor with a reporting relationship to the Vice-President in the Environmental Department. The audit is done for each facility every one to four years depending on need. The audit takes about four days per facility and is usually conducted by a team of one to three people. Checklists are used to guide the audit effort and to identify areas of concern. A formal written report is issued to top management and to the corrective action team. The report contains positive and negative findings as to environmental compliance and recommendations for improvements and timing for the corrective follow-up process. The report is distributed to the facility manager, environmental department manager, manufacturing director, and division vice-president. A draft report is reviewed by the facility and audit personnel at the site upon the conclusion of the audit. Target dates are set for corrective action, and coordinators are assigned for each audit finding that needs corrective action. The corrective actions are tracked using audit computer tracking (ACT) status reports, which are issued on unresolved audit findings every 30 days to the environmental department and to the facility manager until all audit findings are resolved and corrected. Once all the findings are corrected, an audit wrap-up letter is sent to the manufacturing director.

The company is moving from a "compliance-oriented audit" scheme to a proactive environmental man-

agement system (EMS) on a global basis. In 1995, 3M was charged $6,000 (out of a sales of $13 billion) as penalty for environmental non-compliance. In one instance, the company was assessed a penalty of $250,000 for not having the right papers! The need to operate beyond compliance, gain from the process of improving environmental performance, and enhance the resulting corporate reputation has a positive impact on bottom line performance; even so, many influencing factors may not be capable of quantification.

ENVIRONMENTAL MANAGEMENT SYSTEM (EMS)

One of the motives for choosing a proactive Environmental Management System was the need to be customer-oriented. The company wanted their customers to select 3M as their preferred supplier. Through the objective of attaining supply chain excellence, waste reductions in the processes were aimed at delivering the right product at the right time to its customers. The EMS implementation guide was structured to resemble ISO 14000 certification for ease of implementation.

Corporate staff works with facilities to do a "gap analysis" for each element of the EMS and to develop implementation plans. EMS is a facility-driven process, and aggressive time schedules are set for improvements. The different facilities are a collection of companies, and this can lead to differences in implementing EMS practices. Thus, EMS implementation must be facilitated through the formulation of standard operating procedures (SOP) to increase supply chain integration among the different facilities. A summary of the elements of EMS, implementation processes, and results and benefits from EMS are provided:

EMS ELEMENTS	IMPLEMENTATION	RESULTS AND BENEFITS
Regulation and Policies: Identify all regulatory and 3M policy requirements that affect products and operations	Provide guidance to all business units based on individual business needs.	Minimization of 3M's effect on the environment.
Environmental Management Plan: Establish and maintain environmental project plan that defines goals, actions and assignment of responsibilities.	Incorporate environmental challenges and opportunities intro strategic plans and business objectives.	Strategic leveraging of 3M's environmental position and innovative capabilities.
Environmental Operating Procedures: Document operating procedures that achieve and maintain compliance objectives.	Consider the application of the EMS elements at each site of operation.	Improved satisfaction of customer needs.
Environment Assessment: Conduct compliance and system audits to verify performance and identify improvement opportunities.	Obtain assistance and support from Environmental Technology and Safety Department.	Enhanced competitiveness.
Continuous Improvement: Measure and target reductions of waste and emissions, exceed performance expectations, and employ LCM in the identification and satisfaction of customer needs, from product design and manufacture through use and disposition.	Use the implementation guides for EMS and LCM to support the process.	Increased productivity of environmental investments. Facilitation of self-assessment and third-party verification.

The EMS addresses the legal environment-related and internal requirements. A multimedia audit of air, water, and hazardous waste is conducted. The motives for emphasizing environmental audit include the prevention of fines and development of human resources. For example, regulatory agencies such as the EPA and PCA can levy hefty fines even if a single hazardous waste drum is not labeled. The fines can be as high as $1,000 per container. Also, environmental auditing can be used as a training tool. The audits are conducted at the same time in 120 different locations. This enables the tapping of "best practices" and transfer of knowledge gained to other sites that then become part of future training programs. The EMS has implications for supply management. The SOPs help in pointing out variation in raw material quality, which can result in the changing of specifications for raw materials with resulting impact on packaging also. Similarly, quicker detection of waste generation in the operations of suppliers is facilitated.

The environmental audit process flow chart can be used by suppliers to conduct an environmental audit of their own operations, which can also help in developing closer working relationships with suppliers. In an advanced stage of buyer-seller relationship, Suppliers accept packaging materials like storage drums for reconditioning. Also, through JIT purchasing relationships, purchasing can affect the inventory of hazardous material and resulting liability insurance costs.

ENVIRONMENTAL INFORMATION MANAGEMENT

3M's environmental reputation can affect sales, stock price, employee recruitment, and profitability. Preserving a healthy environmental reputation requires a strong environmental program and good communication with markets and customers. The main message in the company's environmental communication conveys awareness of environment-related problems, the constant search for solutions, and progress from learning and then applying the solutions.

The environmental information management program involves direct sharing of information via published media, electronic Intranet, Internet speech meetings, and conferences. Environmental consciousness is also promoted indirectly through awards, recognition, and news stories. The primary target audience for disseminating environmental information includes employees, customers, and shareholders. Communications stress employee contributions to the 3P initiative, simplicity in environmental programs, and a sense of ownership among employees. In a poll of employees conducted by the company, 95 percent of the employees said that 3M was a "good environmental company," and over 90 percent of its employees worldwide said that they had changed their behavior toward the environment since joining the company. Employees can also serve as influential communicators to the general public. Plant managers at 3M are trained for and charged with the responsibility of communicating with their local community.

ENVIRONMENTAL PERFORMANCE SYSTEM

Environmental Policy

The company has the following environmental policy and goals:

- To develop cleaner products and processes
- To work with customers to improve environmental performance of the firm's products
- To disseminate environmental concerns of customers to research and development for solutions
- To invest in pollution-control and pollution-prevention programs globally
- To identify ways of reducing, reusing, or recycling waste materials created during the production process

In order to track its current and future environmental performance, the company sets explicit quantifiable goals. In its Year 2000 goals, the company includes targets for waste reduction and energy conservation (see Figure 7). Through its emphasis on "continuous improvement toward sustainability," using tools such as life-cycle management, the company aims for 50 percent reduction in general of waste, 9 percent reduction in pollution and an annual reduction of 3 percent in energy consumption. A holistic approach is used to reduce waste and conserve energy (see Figures 8 - 10). For example, solvents used in coatings need to be incinerated from time to time. Energy use from the incineration process must be linked to waste generation and release of pollutants. A by-product of the incineration are recovered solvents. Through thermal oxidizers, the solvent waste generated is treated.

In 1995, the company had a goal of 35 percent reduction in environmental releases, and the company achieved a 30 percent reduction the next year. Currently, the company has a goal of 50 percent reduction in waste generation and a goal of 90 percent reduction in releases to the environment. This suggests a need to establish progressive environmental "stretch" goals. In turn, this stretch process motivates employees to take aggressive action, not, just a "point-in-time-effort". The company hopes to achieve zero releases and promote sustainability in the near future. The message to the employees is clear: "Environmental management is everybody's job." Given the aggressive goals for pollution release, purchasing has a responsibility to look for suppliers who can offer the requisite technology to achieve these goals. This also has implications for pricing; the suppliers and the buying firms should know their true cost of waste (COW) in order to facilitate efficient bidding and pricing.

FIGURE 7
YEAR 2000 ENVIRONMENTAL GOALS

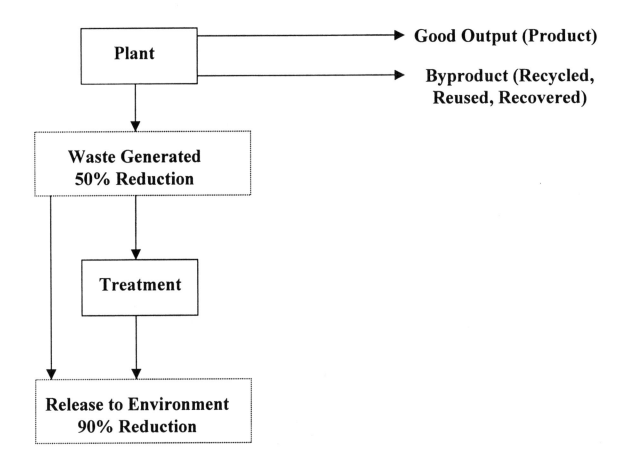

Source: 3M Corporation

FIGURE 8

POTENTIAL SOURCES OF HARMFUL ENVIRONMENTAL EFFECTS AT 3M

Team Formed___ Customer Sampled___
Final Formulation/Construction___
Product Introduction___ Product Maintenance___ Product Withdrawal___

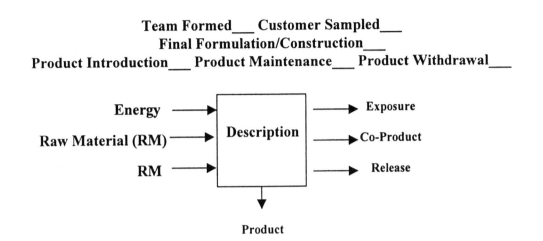

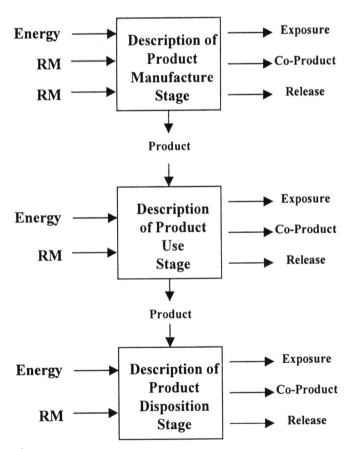

Source:3M Corporation

FIGURE 9
LCM OPPORTUNITY MATRIX

Market Advantage   **Product:**_____   **Date:**_____

	Customer Use	Final Disposal	Materials Acquisition	Manufacture
ENVIRONMENTAL				
---ENERGY **---RESOURCES**				
HEALTH				
SAFETY				

Source: 3M Corporation

FIGURE 10
3M's LCM RISK SCREENING MATRIX

Product ID: _____   Date: _____   Purpose: _____

Milestone: ___ Team Formed ___ Customer Sampled ___ Final Formulation/Construction ___ Product Intro. ___ Maintenance ___ Product Withdrawal

LCM Stages / Env./Hth/Sfty IMPACTS		BEFORE CUSTOMER		Manufacturing			CUSTOMER	
		Material Acquisition	Lab/ Pilot Plant	Process	Packaging	Wrhs, Distrb, Transport	Product Use, Reuse, Maintenance	Disposition (Recycle, Disposal)
		A	B	C	D	E	F	G
ENVIRONMENTAL								
Air	1							
Water	2							
Solid Waste	3							
ENERGY	4							
RESOURCE USE	5							
HEALTH								
Chemical	6							
Noise	7							
Radiation	8							
Ergonomics	9							
SAFETY								
Chemical	10							
Electrical	11							
Mechanical	12							

Legend:
- Impacts understood and Risks adequately addressed
* - Impacts understood but Risks require further attention
? - Impacts/Risks NOT completely understood
(+) - EHS Advantage

Source: 3M Corporation

35

Overall Environmental Performance

Since 1975, the company has developed more than 4,100 pollution prevention projects, eliminating 1.3 million pounds (590 million kilograms) of pollutants and saving more than $710 million. The company invests $150 million a year in environmentally related research and development and an estimated $200 million in environmental operations worldwide. Since 1990, the company has invested $175 million worldwide in pollution control equipment to reduce air emissions. In 1994, 3M achieved an estimated 50-percent reduction in all releases to the air, water, and land, and reduced waste 21 percent.

The company lays out aggressive future-oriented targets for specific environmental goals in multiple categories (see Figure 11). For example, one current goal is to reduce all releases to air, water and land by 90 percent and to reduce generation of waste 50 percent by the year 2000, based on 1990 levels. Ultimately, the company's goal is to approach zero release levels. In the area of air emissions, the company's goals are to reduce releases to air 90 percent by the year 2000, using 1990 as the base year. The company reduced worldwide air emissions by 70 percent from about 160 million pounds (72 million kilograms) in 1989 to less than 45 million pounds (20 million kilograms) in 1993. The company also installed more than 30 pollution control units in their facilities around the world at a cost of $175 million.

In the area of water emissions, the company's goals are to reduce releases to water 90 percent by the year 2000, using 1990 as the base year. The company reduced U.S. water releases 90 percent from about 5 million pounds (2 million kilograms) annually in 1987 to less than 0.2 million pounds (0.9 million kilograms) in 1994.

For waste reduction, the company's goals are to reduce waste generation 35 percent by 1995 and 50 percent by the year 2000. The company reduced worldwide waste 21 percent by 1993 from 1990 levels. During 1993, the U.S. operations recovered and sold almost 199 million pounds (90 million kilograms) of paper, plastics, solvents, metals and other byproducts. This is an increase of 31 percent over 1990 levels of more than 150 million pounds (68 million kilograms). The amount of solid waste sent to landfills in the U.S. decreased 30 percent from 283 million pounds (127 million kilograms) in 1990 to 198 million pounds (89 million kilograms) in 1993.

In the area of energy consumption, the company seeks to improve energy efficiency 20 percent per unit of production or per square foot of office and warehouse space by 1995, using 1990 as the base year. U.S. non-manufacturing operations have reduced energy usage by 9 percent. However, worldwide energy use in manufacturing has increased 3 percent per unit of production primarily because of the installation of energy-intensive air pollution control equipment and lower-than-anticipated production levels. The company has had an energy management program since 1973. From 1973 to 1993, the company has improved its efficiency about 56 percent, with production tripling in that period, and energy usage increasing by only 20 percent. The company has also avoided an estimated 4.2 billion pounds (1.9 billion kilograms) of air pollutant emissions such as carbon dioxide and carbon monoxide. A major effort is under way to educate employees in ways to reduce energy usage. For example, administrative employees reduce energy usage by turning off lights, copiers, computers and other equipment when they are not needed.

In the area of developing environmentally friendly products, the goal for the company is to develop products and processes that have a minimal environmental impact. To achieve this goal, the company spends 15 percent of research and development or $150 million annually to reduce the environmental impact of new and existing products and manufacturing processes. This has resulted in more than 100 major new or improved products. Packaging is an important component of developing environmentally friendly products. Within the last two years, the company has reduced packaging on products by 8 million pounds. The Environmental Marketing Claims Review program was introduced in 1990 to maintain a consistent approach to product and environmental issues worldwide. All environmental marketing claims made by the company must be substantiated and communicated in writing to prevent misunderstanding.

ENVIRONMENTAL ORGANIZATION STRUCTURE

The organizational structure for environmental affairs at 3M is given in Figure 12. A separate environmental department reporting to top management is indicative of the importance attached to environmental issues. The centralized organizational structure for the environmental department (environmental professionals are not in plant but in corporate offices) has the advantages of consistency in decisions, efficiency, and ease of transferring knowledge gained from solving similar problems in several plants. To reap these advantages, top management commitment to environmental issues is critical. The corporate environmental structure is lean, with fewer employees and lower expenditures on overhead that have resulted in increased flexibility in manufacturing. Administrative costs are saved because less time is required to obtain permits, and faster changes are realized.

Employee issues are important for becoming environmentally conscious. Individual responsibility for environmental actions as opposed to a corporate prerogative is emphasized. For example, in 3M, *each employee,*

FIGURE 11

BASIC FRAMEWORK ELEMENTS OF
ENVIRONMENTAL QUALITY SYSTEM

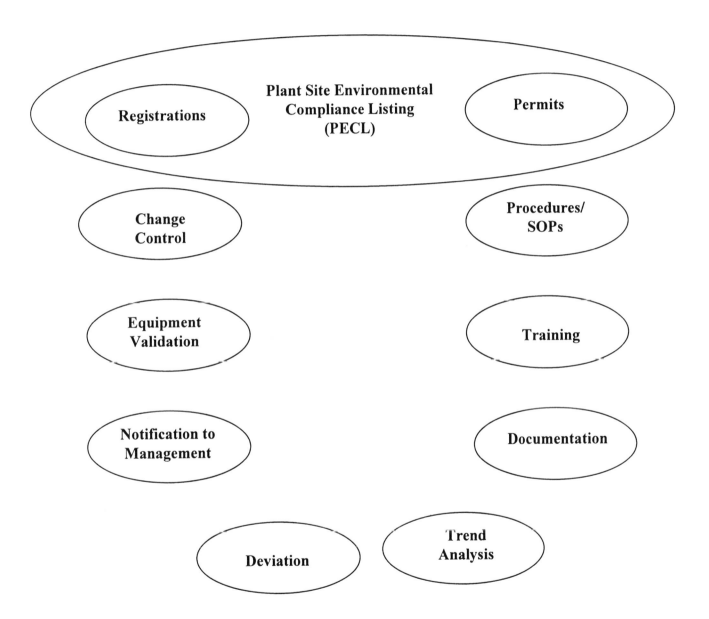

Source: 3M Corporation

FIGURE 12

ORGANIZATION CHART OF ENVIRONMENTAL DEPARTMENT

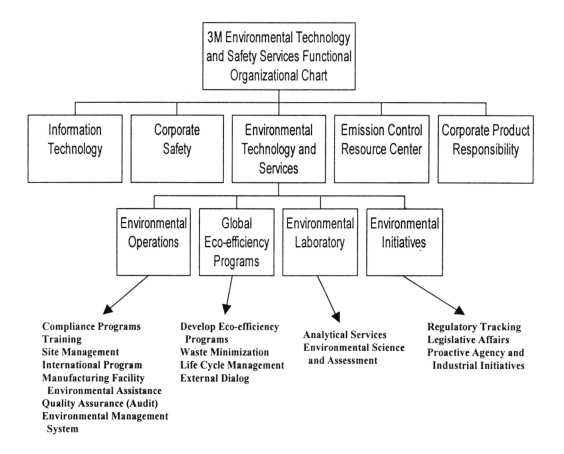

Source: 3M Corporation

not just corporate staff, is responsible for pollution prevention. Rather than just offering suggestions, employees are empowered to act in response to environmental problems. The company reward structure also emphasizes results. Similarly, superior environmental performance is recognized. Divisions that pursue the highest number of environmental projects are accorded recognition. Other practices include presenting a leadership award given for actions or projects that best exemplify the company's environmental posture. If potential benefits from these actions or projects to the local community, then they are pursued even if there is no direct impact on the company.

LESSONS LEARNED

The key lessons learned from this case study are summarized as follows:

- An early emphasis on environmental issues is important — 3M started as early as in 1960!

- Top management commitment to environmental issues is critical. For example, a separate environmental department reporting to the top management indicates the importance attached to environmental issues by the company.

- Employee issues are an important part of becoming environmentally conscious. At 3M, employees are empowered to act in response to environmental problems, rather than simply for offering suggestions. The reward structure also emphasizes results.

- Synergy between the company's strong environmental image/reputation and its environmentally sensitive products is important.

- A holistic approach, such as supply chain integration, to environmental management links reduction in energy consumption to waste generation and release of pollutants. Using a customer-driven environmental management system along with standard operating procedures facilitates supply chain integration.

- Setting aggressive and progressive environmental goals is important

- Using tools such as LCM and environmental audits improves environmental and operating performance. Suppliers are asked to keep track of their COW so that these can be reduced. Supplier negotiations and selection revolve around COW and other environmental issues.

DAIMLER BENZ, AG

COMPANY BACKGROUND

Daimler-Benz is a German auto manufacturer of Mercedes-Benz luxury cars, jet and motor vehicle engines, heavy-duty trucks, and buses. Corporate headquarters are in Stuttgart, Germany. Daimler-Benz was formed in 1926 by the merger of two pioneering German automobile companies, one founded by Carl Benz, the other by Gottlieb Daimler.

From its inception, Mercedes-Benz has viewed its supply base as critical for survival in an intensively competitive industry. This perception has over the years developed into a supplier-teaming program called TANDEM drawn directly from the corporate principles of Mercedes-Benz.

MERCEDES-BENZ CORPORATE PRINCIPLES

The company's core statement, "Mercedes-Benz — Your Guiding Star," stands for a progressive way of thinking and relates to corporate conduct. In an in-depth dialogue with their staff, Mercedes-Benz developed from the core statement five corporate principles which affect daily activities and their relationships with suppliers (TANDEM). These five corporate principles are:

1. "We make customers enthusiastic about the three-pointed star."

2. "We want to be the best in terms of innovation, quality and profitability."

3. "We are actively pursuing an open-minded culture."

4. "We integrate our business partners."

5. "We assume ecological responsibility."

TANDEM — Shaping the Future Together

Retaining international competitiveness in a climate of rapid change requires strategic reorientation on the part of both manufacturers and suppliers in the automotive industry. Today, more than ever, the quality and success of a product depend on the competence and performance of the supplying industry.

In order to ensure future success, it is not enough to simply accept changes resulting from market dynamics — a firm must actively initiate them. The entire supply chain must embrace a process of ongoing change, and the willingness to change became a competitive tool.

Having learned by experience that these market challenges can be handled best through teamwork, Mercedes-Benz took a new approach toward teamwork with their supply base in 1993 — it was called the TANDEM alliance. According to their corporate principles, the TANDEM objective is to join forces with their supply base in order to mutually survive the rigors and dynamics of the marketplace and shape their destiny together. To achieve this goal, it is necessary to subject products and processes to continuous critical analysis at every stage of the value-added process. The results are custom-tailored concepts to reduce costs, provide consumer benefits and improve environmental protection, while ensuring optimum product quality.

Mercedes-Benz alliance partners are progressive companies that set for themselves the highest standards of performance. Dedication to total quality management principles is just as much a given as a holistic view and high innovation readiness. Through mutual trust, two-way communication, and early integration of suppliers in all decisions affecting them, Mercedes-Benz and their suppliers jointly lay the foundation for a functioning alliance.

To represent the framework of this alliance philosophy into concretion, Mercedes-Benz built an "activity house" of many rooms, supported by the pillars "Events," "Organization," and "Information". A diagram of the Mercedes- Benz alliance "activity house" is presented in Figure 13. Only if each supplier identifies with TANDEM can the concept function effectively, only if the shared philosophy of TANDEM is applied in day-to-day operations can long-term effective cooperation come about.

More than 800 successful projects in the first three years of TANDEM demonstrate the success of the program. These experiences give Mercedes-Benz reason for optimism and provide motivation to meet future challenges. The signposts of the future are clearly marked with regard to customer satisfaction, quality, **the environment,** and competitive positioning.

TANDEM — Principles

Identification with a mutual philosophy and the pursuit of mutual goals are the basis for long-term cooperation within the TANDEM alliance. The greater the Mercedes-Benz performance the longer the commitment.

Mercedes-Benz highly values the professionalism and the work of their TANDEM partners and provides an open arena for creativity, initiative and enterprise; to include critical questioning of even Mercedes-Benz performance.

To enable TANDEM to prove its merits in day-to-day operations, ongoing dialogue and systematic long-term cooperation are essential. This involves a wealth of new experiences and impetus for all parties.

The TANDEM principles are:

1. Together we will be instrumental in creating a rewarding future.

2. Our conduct and our products focus on the customer's needs and expectations. This customer driven approach gives us distinct competitive advantages.

3. Performance-driven companies will become our partners if they identify with our philosophy.

4. We expect and encourage the creativity and initiative of our suppliers.

5. We target the utmost in cost consciousness; for mutual benefit.

6. The teamwork to which we aspire is of a long-term nature.

7. We put a premium on fairness and information transfer in a business relationship based on mutual trust.

EVENTS: TANDEM — Plenum

Meeting in plenum are the senior executives of the supplying industry and of the Mercedes-Benz research and development, operating units, and purchasing departments. There the firms lay the foundation for joint efforts and identify opportunities afforded by the alliance organization structure.

Mercedes-Benz feels that such events are the appropriate platform to formulate joint entrepreneurial mission statements. Here the focus is on discussion of current and strategic matters of cooperation, as well as what the automotive market demands of the industry. The consensus reached establishes the direction for work on products and processes. Plenum meetings also provide an opportunity to present exemplary projects and achievements to all TANDEM partners.

EVENTS: TANDEM — Forum

As the need arises, workshops for specialists are held several times annually in TANDEM forum. Together the partners discuss specific matters of relevance to Mercedes-Benz and develop intelligent solutions based on detailed first-hand information. The intensity of the partnership is demonstrated by the fact that more than 24 forums were held in the first three years of this alliance.

FIGURE 13
DAIMLER BENZ ALLIANCE ACTIVITY HOUSE

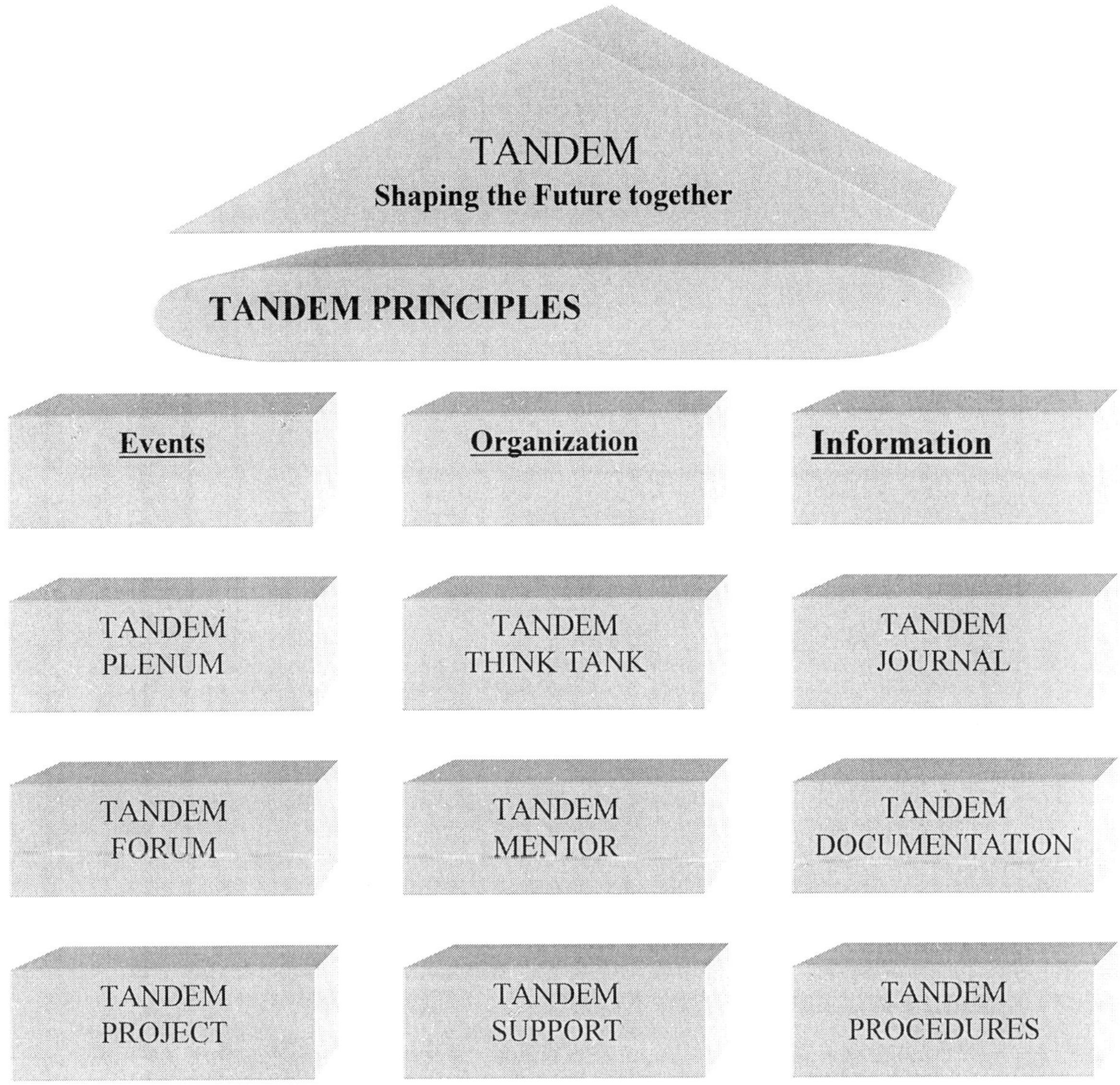

TANDEM
Shaping the Future together

TANDEM PRINCIPLES

Events	Organization	Information
TANDEM PLENUM	TANDEM THINK TANK	TANDEM JOURNAL
TANDEM FORUM	TANDEM MENTOR	TANDEM DOCUMENTATION
TANDEM PROJECT	TANDEM SUPPORT	TANDEM PROCEDURES

Products, processes, and functions systematically and clearly categorize the content emphasis of the forum. In product-related forums, objectives, missions and important milestones are the focus of discussions by specialists from supplier companies, as well as participating Mercedes-Benz departments. Additionally, this cooperation makes it possible to further develop contacts and communication among suppliers.

Mercedes-Benz also integrates their suppliers at an early stage in configuring mutual business processes. CAD/CAM strategy, quality management and **recycling** are only three examples of subjects treated in the TANDEM forum. Strategies, concepts and instruments of individual corporate functions are likewise made public and explained in forum for interested partners.

EVENTS: TANDEM — Project

TANDEM projects are the building blocks of the "activity house" in which mutual cooperation most clearly affects the operating results. In small teams, suppliers and Mercedes-Benz staff work together on concrete projects. In keeping with demanding, mutually arrived at target agreements, Mercedes-Benz and their suppliers form a roundtable and seek innovative solutions. Interaction of participants is effectively supported by clear ground rules. The emphasis here is on supplier parts for current models and new development projects, capital goods and precisely defined processes.

In addition to enhancing commercial success, project activities enable the suppliers to present and demonstrate their full capabilities. Positive results build motivation, dedication and receptiveness to new ideas.

ORGANIZATION: TANDEM — Think Tank

In making the most of existing structures, spontaneous ideas are often just as important as strategic considerations. That is why the TANDEM think tank is open to all suggestions and proposals from suppliers as a type of "mailbox."

During day-to-day operations, the suppliers gain insights into Mercedes-Benz work structures and processes. Potential for improvement is often discovered in areas such as direct product costs through functional, design and material-related optimization, or enhancing sequences and systems both qualitatively and quantitatively.

ORGANIZATION: TANDEM — Mentor

For problems and questions beyond day-to-day work processes, suppliers may contact a point person in the Mercedes-Benz purchasing department. As a mentor s/he handles questions of cooperation and supports the supplier on cross-functional problem complexes. The point person also mediates if there is any discrepancy between TANDEM philosophy or principles and actual experiences.

These mentor relationships ensure ongoing dialogues with the people in supplier companies. Additionally, mentors are charged with the task of clarifying issues arising in day-to-day cooperation, addressing and clarifying topics of an interdepartmental nature and serving as moderators in solution processes. The TANDEM mentors, however, have no influence on either designation of suppliers, or decisions concerning operational business issues with suppliers.

ORGANIZATION: TANDEM — Support

In TANDEM support, Mercedes-Benz gives the supplying industry access to company know-how and special expertise in order to be able to achieve jointly established goals and complete defined projects.

Supplier support can be provided, for example, in such areas as quality management, supply chain optimization, and **environmental protection,** as well as matters of planning technology and business administration.

The supplier accesses support by presenting explicit questions, which are then communicated specifically to the responsible departments. Mercedes-Benz handles these questions with confidentiality and seeks solutions together with suppliers on-site.

INFORMATION: TANDEM - Journal

With the magazine *TANDEM-Journal,* Mercedes Benz provides their suppliers with regular, event-related information on all activities covered by the cooperation concept. In interviews and articles on events or actual projects, Mercedes-Benz furnishes detailed background information on all TANDEM building blocks, takes stock, and presents insightful articles on individual projects. The journal reports on the latest activities and encourages exchange of experience.

With the *TANDEM-journal* Mercedes-Benz and its suppliers have jointly created a medium which not only documents the successful cooperation but also continues to stimulate intensive dialogue.

INFORMATION: TANDEM — Documentation

The documentation serves to communicate professional topics to the broadest possible audience within supplier companies. In this way, discussion of timely issues can be continued and intensified in the field, beyond Plenum and Forum. The documentation is distributed to the various workshop participants and, additionally, made available by request through the journal.

INFORMATION: TANDEM — Procedures

The alliance structure to which Mercedes-Benz aspires is based on clearly defined ground rules that spell out the nature of the cooperation. For this reason, TANDEM procedures contain important information and policies governing concrete questions of operational cooperation.

With a minimum of rules, Mercedes-Benz systematizes those procedures that must be uniform. In this way, they provide the parameters for creative processes and missions. In TANDEM procedures, Mercedes-Benz describes and updates the contents whenever they feel they have learned something new of value from the alliance experiences.

The TANDEM Outlook and Environmental Sensitivity

In TANDEM, Mercedes-Benz has rapidly achieved successes that they had not considered possible at the start of this new supplier alliance system. Despite the favorable results, much work must be completed. The dynamics of competition; they dare not add one penny more to the cost of a vehicle due to environmental sensitivity, are destined to further increase in the years to come. But it is precisely this that gives Mercedes-Benz an opportunity to candidly and actively continue on the path of environmental effectiveness. For Mercedes-Benz has learned that environmental effectiveness often translates into cost savings. These goal-oriented activities will make it possible for Mercedes-Benz to expand the competitiveness of their products, thus further improving their market share.

For their specific suppliers, this means that Mercedes-Benz will be integrating them still earlier in product design, processes and strategic missions. The earlier the supplier involvement in designs, the quicker and more effective accomplishment of environmental goals. This will also help the suppliers become more competitive and maintain or even expand their supply scope. In addition, a separate part of each request for proposal (RFP) includes environmental issues. For example which material, percentage of recyclable material, percentage product waste, and recycling plan for that waste is solicited for every part. Also, in the product development conceptual phase, a distinct part of the process is the development of a product environmental life-cycle strategy. This life-cycle strategy drives environmental efforts through the entire life of the product, including return and recycling.

Mercedes-Benz has, through experience, found that environmental considerations are expensive unless introduced early in the conceptual design phase. For these reasons, Mercedes-Benz sees it as vitally important to constantly reexamine their understanding of partnership. Mercedes-Benz is convinced that the key to future success lies in cooperation throughout the supply chain.

LESSONS LEARNED

- Change should be viewed as a competitive tool and environmental efficiency viewed as a positive catalyst for change.

- Products and processes should be subjected to continual critical analysis at every stage of the value-added process.

- The early integration of suppliers into all decisions affecting them is critical to environmental effectiveness.

- The close alignment of supplier capabilities with Daimler Benz environmental goals was critical to program success. This alignment is achieved through an alliance supporting organizational and informational framework and the benchmarking of performance with environmental, quality, and cost parameters.

DEKRA UMWELT GMBH

COMPANY BACKGROUND

DEKRA was founded in 1925 in Berlin as a registered organization. It combined vehicle fleets and other companies operating commercial vehicles. The task of its engineers was to carry out regular checks on the vehicles of the organization members in order to identify defects in good time and to provide an independent estimate of the costs of any repairs.

Services dealing with every aspect of the motor vehicle, its roadworthiness and economic use, formed and still form the focus of DEKRA's work. Over the course of years these services have been consistently expanded and supplemented by new areas of work.

DEKRA TODAY

Today, some 20 different companies operate under the umbrella of DEKRA e. V. DEKRA subsidiaries and affiliated companies in Germany and throughout the rest of Europe offer a wide range of services. They carry out testing and provide certification, advice, reports, and training. DEKRA's name has become synonymous with high reliability, economy, and quality of life.

BUSINESS UNITS OF DEKRA

1. Environmental Protection Experts

- Materials flow management
- Damage assessment
- Redevelopment planning and monitoring of ground and buildings
- Waste water management
- Hazardous waste management
- Assessment and ongoing surveillance of industrial plants

2. Environmental Testing Stations

- Contaminated Land, Air, Water, Noise
- Emission measurements and air control, predictions, and expert reports
- Calculations on the spreading of harmful chemicals
- Drawing up licensing procedures
- Installation consulting
- Functionality testing and calibration of atmospheric gauges
- Environmental meteorology
- Expertise on noise abatement
- Hazardous Substances
- Analysis of working areas under environmental decrees
- Analysis of indoor quality
- Material analysis

3. Laboratory

Laboratory Measurements and Analysis

- Wood preserver
- Ground and water pollution
- Hazardous waste
- Fire remains
- Cleansing agents
- Gauging of asbestos fiber concentration

Certification of Environmentally Friendly Products

- Engine oil
- Radiator protection
- Cleansing agent

4. Eco-management

- Strategic environmental consulting
- EU-regulation (EWG) No. 1836/93
- ISO 14000 (Environment)
- ISO 9000 (Quality)
- ISO 17000 (Safety)
- Audits, health and safety, and risk analysis
- Environmental controlling and anti-pollution cost management
- Validation of environmental management systems under European decree, Environmental Management and Audit Scheme (EMAS)
- Certification of environmental management systems under international standards

5. Safety Management

- On-the-Job Safety
- Health and safety audits and implementation of safety management systems
- Experts on on-the-job safety under international standards
- Safety engineering consulting including consulting on fire prevention and on ergonomic workplaces
- Safety training
- Safety Engineering Inspection
- Playgrounds
- Amenity facilities
- Sports equipment

EMAS — A CURRENT EUROPEAN STANDARD

On June 29, 1993, the Council of the European Union passed the EEC-No. 1836/93; the regulation is known as EMAS, which stands for Environmental Management and Audit Scheme. In Germany, the regulation is known as "Oko-Audit." The aim of EMAS is a continuous improvement of environmental performance through an environmental management system and environmental audits.

Participation in EMAS is totally voluntary and the ordinance does not contain any requirements or bans. The aim is for exclusively economic incentives to be the instigator for the introduction of an environmental management system. However, participants must commit themselves to an appropriate continuous improvement of environmental performance; for example, companies must reduce the effects on the environment to the extent achievable with the help of economically viable applications of the best available technology. In other words, more will be done in these companies than would be required on the basis of the latest state-of-the-art technology.

SIX REASONS FOR PARTICIPATING IN EMAS:

1. COST SAVINGS

End-of-pipe measures are becoming increasingly more expensive: each reduction in pollutants — over and above the latest state-of-the-art technology — of a few parts-per-million requires a very high outlay for technology and consequently high investment costs. Environmental management identifies weaknesses, in good time, where cost-saving measures can use avoidance strategies or recycling systems.

2. RISK PRECAUTIONS

Environmental management highlights potential environmental hazards and provides clarity regarding the law of liability. Accordingly, taking appropriate precautions to prevent risk can minimize a risk.

3. SITE SAFEGUARDS

Communication with the general public in the form of an environmental statement increases the acceptance of the operating site by the neighboring population and local authorities. It is also intended to achieve a more rapid implementation of licensing procedures and greater self-responsibility due to reduced official supervision.

4. ENHANCED IMAGE

Environmental protection is an important sales argument. Participation in EMAS can provide competitive advantages on the sales front.

5. EMPLOYEE MOTIVATION

Participation in EMAS promotes employee identification with the company and consequently motivates them to improve their performance.

6. CONDITIONS OF SUPPLY

Industry challenges its suppliers to participate in EMAS by including only those who operate registered sites on their list of suppliers. Government authorities will also take the same approach when issuing public contracts.

THE ROUTE IS THE OBJECTIVE

The route to obtaining the environmental approved certification symbol is through the establishment of an environmental policy by the company management, an initial review by internal experts, and the specification of environmental objectives and programs (see Figure 14).

The public is provided with the following information in an environmental statement:

1. The environmental policy and the environmental program

2. Specific data on emissions, sewage pollution and waste management, together with technical documentation

Accredited environmental verifiers check to see whether the EMAS standards are being maintained, examine the accuracy of the environmental statement, and validate the system. They then notify the competent agency — in Germany that is the Chamber of Trade and Industry — that the operational site is an EMAS participant. This Chamber of Trade and Industry in turn checks to see whether any concerns have been expressed by the authorities against the company and then includes this site in the published list of all companies participating in the EMAS. The company can now use their statement of participation. By carrying out regular environmental audits the company ensures that the environmental management system is applied. Every three years the verifier checks for continuous improvement of environmental performance, and the validity of the statement of participation is then extended.

ACCREDITATION SYSTEM

Accredited environmental verifiers (see Figure 15) have to meet a demanding profile of requirements. This includes technical and sector-specific knowledge, neutrality and reliability. These requirements are checked and monitored in Germany by the accreditation body DAU (Deutsche Akkreditierungs - und Zulassungsgesellschaft fur Umweltgutachter). An environmental verification committee called UGA (Umweltgutachterausschub) lays down the guidelines for licensing and the assessment guidelines for the supervision of the verifiers. This committee is made up of six members from the industry, four members of the environmental verifiers, nine members of the federal and state governments, three members from the trade unions, and three members from the environmental groups.

In Germany there are currently about 60 verifiers and 10 verifier organizations accredited, and about 100 companies have their statement of participation. Soon companies that have sites in and outside of Europe will adopt a new combination between EMAS and ISO 14001. Another trend is very clear: the public sector and the service industries (such as banks, insurance companies, and hospitals) will also implement the environmental management system.

LESSONS LEARNED

The operation of industrial plants is fraught with environmental risks. Since environmental liability laws came into force, these risks have caused a serious struggle for survival for many companies. They are facing considerable environmental liability risks and insurance companies have little desire to insure such risks.

Many operating entities have a minimal awareness of accidental risks and their consequences evolving from the normal operations of their plants and equipment. This is regarded as a serious problem by the insurance industry that offers environmental liability insurance for industrial plants. Owing to economic considerations and negative experiences with environmental liability cases, insurance companies have little tendency to insure environmental liability risks as long as their type and potential magnitude are not foreseeable. Therefore, insufficiently informed operating entities may find themselves in the unenviable position of not receiving the environmental insurance needed or receiving it at a prohibitive cost. A screening and testing of environmental risks seem essential.

This auditing of environmental risks enables the firm to quickly and systematically comprehend and uniformly classify environmental risks created by industrial operations. Such a risk-audit procedure would evaluate hazardous potentials within the operation and classify them using a uniform parameter. Insurers could then calculate the environmental liability law policies realistically.

A company that uses a risk-auditing procedure has precise information concerning potential "weak points" in the process and their potential hazardous impact. This audit forms an optimal basis for targeted improvements of safety standards and usually helps reduce insurance premiums considerably.

Without an effective auditing procedure, the steps involved in the calculation of an environmental insurance policy premium were disadvantageous for both parties. The environmental risks relating to a particular plant had to be estimated and classified using pre-established tariff scales. The circumstances surrounding each particular situation were ignored for the most part, even

FIGURE 14
ROUTE TO OBTAINING EMAS ENVIRONMENTAL APPROVAL

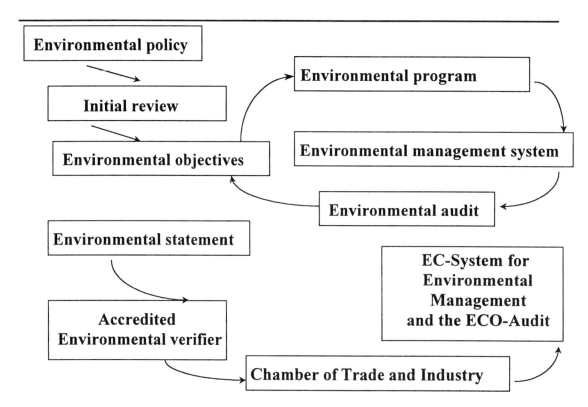

though the particulars are of prime importance in the calculation of potential environmental risks. For example, the unique technology used in a plant, as well as the meticulous safety procedures, was often left out of any calculations. With the implementation of a self-realized risk audit procedure, parameters can be used that enable an extensive, individual, and objective risk assessment.

THE AUDIT PROCEDURE

The environmental hazards caused by an operating entity can be classified simply:

1. The hazardous potential created by the substances used with the operating entity
2. The potential for operating failures within the plant
3. The safety precautions for these causes

First, the environmental audit must identify the kind and amount of relevant environmental substances used within the operation. In addition, any further hazardous substances created during a process failure must be identified. The experts attempt to clarify:

1. Which failures are to be expected
2. Probability of these failures
3. What the causes might be

Also, these perceptions can be classified into minor, moderate, and high potential failures, as well as into various predefined categories of failures and their effects. This means that within the lowest category of effects, only existing hazardous substances reach and affect the outside environment. Within the highest risk category, there are additional threats of secondary damages to the environment due to closely located environmentally hazardous materials.

A "worst case" scenario analysis must be performed. During this "worst case" scenario analysis the existence and effectiveness of technical safety policies and procedures can be evaluated. Policies and safety procedures at the facility can be classified into three categories similar to the classification schema used for the hazard potential. The combining of the three failure possibility categories with the three safety categories leads to an order of nine possible safety classifications which describe the environmental standard of the facility.

Such an environmental risk auditing procedure can be developed into a MIS-supported expert system. The audit will not only assist in developing realistic insurance potential liabilities and rate tariffs for the firm, but will also provide a plan of continuous improvement that can be benchmarked across plant and division.

FIGURE 15

ACCREDITATION SYSTEM FOR ENVIRONMENTAL VERIFIERS AND CERTIFICATION BODIES PURSUANT TO THE EMAS-REGULATION OF 1993 AND ENVIRONMENTAL AUDIT ACT OF 1995

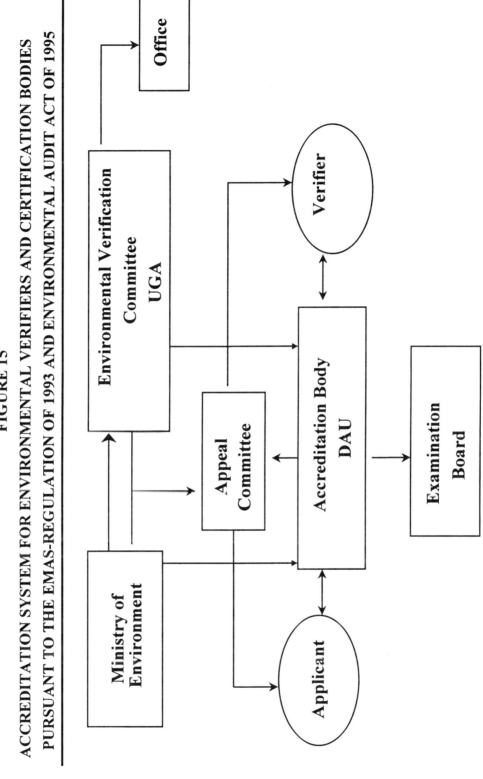

DENSO MANUFACTURING MICHIGAN, INC.

COMPANY BACKGROUND

Denso Corporation, the global parent company for Denso Manufacturing Michigan, Inc., was founded in 1949. Despite being a relatively young company, Denso has grown rapidly, especially in automotive electronics, and now has sales of over 1.2 trillion yen.[1] The company headquarters are in Kariya, which is about 20 kilometers southeast of Nagoya, Japan.

Over 40,000 people work at various Denso locations, which center around their headquarters in Kariya, and include 11 plants, and 21 branch and sales offices in Japan. Denso is a truly global operation with 42 overseas companies and 9 sales offices in 21 countries besides Japan. The Denso Sales Composition is shown in Figure 16 and the Denso Earnings per Share are provided in Figure 17.

COMPANY SUMMARY

Established - December 16, 1949

Japanese plants - 11

Overseas companies - 41

Overseas offices - 9

Capital (March 31, 1996) - 112.2 billion Yen

Net sales (April 1, 1995 — March 31, 1996)
Non-consolidated basis - 1,230.4 billion Yen
Consolidated basis - 1,422.6 billion Yen

Net income (April 1, 1995 — March 31, 1996)
Non-consolidated basis - 69.6 billion Yen
Consolidated basis - 89.8 billion Yen

Employees (March 31, 1996)
Non-consolidated basis - 40,800
Consolidated basis - 56,300

The Denso philosophy has three major components. The mission of the firm is to contribute to a better world by creating value together with a vision for the future. Their management principles are to ensure customer satisfaction through quality products and services, to attain global growth through anticipation of change, to foster environmental preservation and harmony with society, and to maintain corporate vitality and respect for individuality. The individual spirit of the employees is to be creative in thought and steady in action, to be cooperative and pioneering, and to be trustworthy by improving oneself.

Denso holds a leadership position in technologies that maximize vehicle safety and minimize the environmental impact of automobiles. Denso commits 7 to 8 percent of total annual sales revenue for research and development. Of Denso's 9,400 engineers worldwide, 5,000 dedicate themselves to research and development. Research and development drives their technological innovations, which in turn generates the cycle of new products. High performance, safety, and fuel efficiency have long been high priorities in the design of automobiles for Denso, and over the years this list of priorities has grown to include consideration for societal needs and the environment.

Denso has been a North American manufacturer for more than 20 years, with North American customer relationships for more than 30 years. Denso manufacturing facilities operate on a foundation of continuous improvement. No matter how small a process, it is a powerful link to another process. The result is a network of carefully researched methods for achieving superior results. Few manufacturers go to the extremes of scrutiny and testing as Denso. State-of-the-art equipment enables their quality departments to confirm critical details. Denso also uses machine vision inspection systems to ensure the quality of products. *Industry Week* magazine in 1996 named Denso Manufacturing Michigan, Inc. one of the 10 best manufacturing firms in the United States.

DENSO PROCUREMENT

Denso Manufacturing Michigan purchases more than $500 million per year in goods and services from 86 suppliers. The plant runs at 80 percent local content suppliers; local being defined as U.S.-based suppliers. The remaining 20 percent is primarily composed of material production viewed as too environmentally damaging to produce in the U.S. The Japanese view toward environmental issues seems odd; individually, they are quite environmentally sensitive, but less so from a corporate perspective. Environmental issues have historically not driven product innovation. In fact, the management of Denso Manufacturing Michigan has experienced a very conservative response to product and process change suggestions driven by environmental issues. Where change has occurred, it was driven either by cost savings and/or customer satisfaction. For example, the change in the HVAC core to aluminum from copper-brass removed the need for cosmetic painting which saved $ .20 per unit not including a significant reduction in environmental costs due to elimination of the painting. As another example, a special coating of water shedding paint which kills-off bacteria was added because of customer complaints concerning a musty smell when the A/C unit was turned on. This painting added nearly $1.00 per unit. These examples highlight the need at Denso to carefully

[1] Exchange rate (WSJ) as of March 25, 1997 was 123.71 yen per U.S. dollar.

FIGURE 16

DENSO SALES COMPOSITION

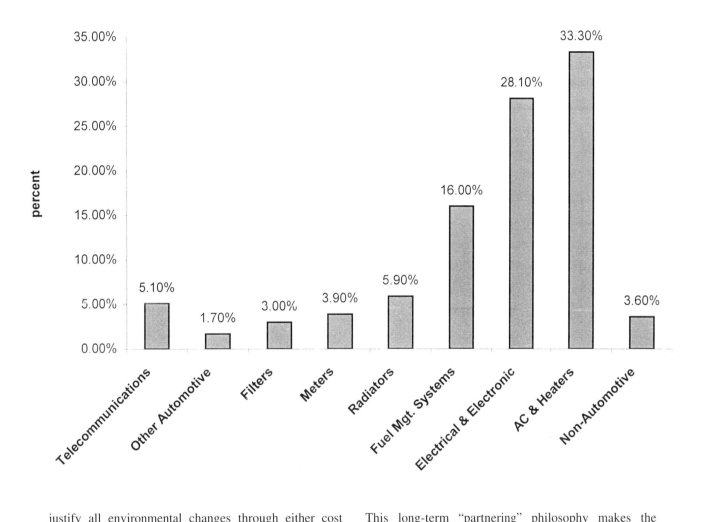

justify all environmental changes through either cost reduction or customer satisfaction issues.

Denso has discovered that having a "tradition" in the supply chain can be damaging to environmental effectiveness and innovation. There can develop a resistance to change and a "don't like to try this first" mentality. It takes a supplier, on average, in excess of two years to become certified at Denso. Concurrently, supplier change is very difficult; at least a two year process.

This long-term "partnering" philosophy makes the incorporation of technological innovations by a new supplier difficult. The role of the buyer must increasingly include continual environmental scanning for new innovations and persuading the existing supply base to adopt and develop these new technologies. For example, Denso attempted to persuade their existing supplier of solvent-based paint to develop the capability to manufacture powder-based paint for several years before the central engineering group at Denso mandated the

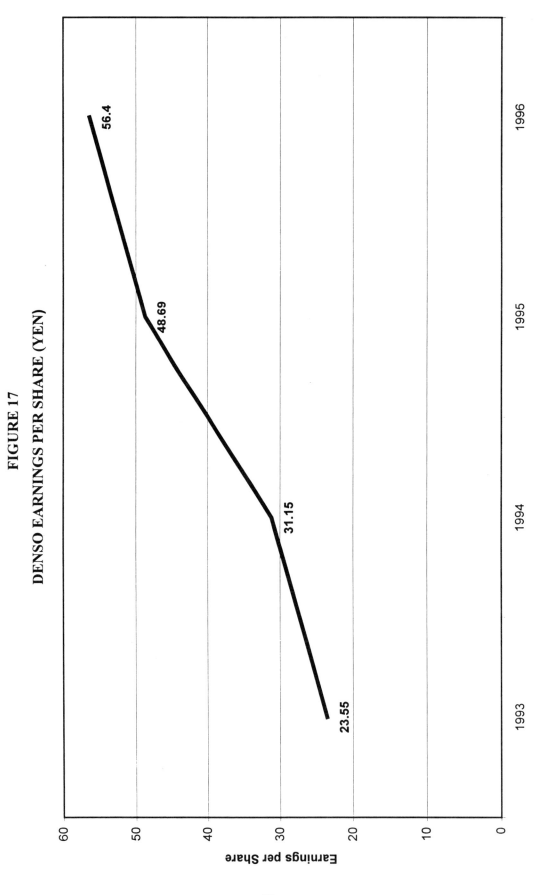

FIGURE 17

DENSO EARNINGS PER SHARE (YEN)

56.4

48.69

31.15

23.55

Earnings per Share

1993   1994   1995   1996

50

change. In a similar manner, Denso purchasing is already exhorting their supply based to prepare for ISO 14000 certification, which they see as inevitable.

A key driver of environmental change has been the waste disposal budgeting process. The waste disposal budget is not charged to any one department to keep it separate from the inevitable budget cutting process. Yet, control of the budget has been assigned to procurement to ensure the cross-functional linkages and communication between the three key departmental players. Those departments are human resources, which controls safety issues and policy; process engineering, which controls the environmental processing issues; and purchasing, which controls the supply chain management issues (such as waste disposal site certification).

A key component of Denso's environmental initiatives is the meticulous tracking of all waste, labor, material, time, etc. Because of this policy many changes which simultaneously reduced waste and cost while improving environmental effectiveness have been made.

LESSONS LEARNED

- Carefully justify all environmental changes through either cost reduction or customer satisfaction issues.

- The focus of continuous improvement used so effectively during TQM program implementation can be applied quite effectively to improving environmental efficiency and effectiveness.

ELI LILLY

COMPANY BACKGROUND

Eli Lilly and Company is a global pharmaceutical corporation with products sold in 156 countries. It has approximately 29,000 employees. In 1996, it had net sales of $7.4 billion and a net income of $1.5 billion. Its annual research and development expenditures average $1.2 billion, which is 16 percent of sales. The average cost of developing a new drug for this company is around $400 million, with an average of 15 years from discovery to use by patient.

The company is focusing on the discovery and development of the most effective pharmaceutical-based healthcare solutions for its diverse customers throughout the world. There is a distinct emphasis on accelerating drug discovery and development processes in order to increase the speed at which new products achieve regulatory approval and reach patients. To achieve this goal, the company pursues innovation through the creative combination of scientific discovery and application of information technology. Among its most popular drugs

are: Humulin, human insulin, the world's first human-healthcare product created using recombinant DNA technology; Prozac, the world's most widely prescribed anti-depressant; and Ceclor, a member of the cephalosporin family that became the world's top-selling antibiotic.

Eli Lilly uses strategic alliances to obtain cost-effective means of building its capabilities in pharmaceutical innovation. The company engages in a wide variety of collaborative research arrangements with universities and biotechnology companies. Currently, Eli Lilly has approximately 35 alliances with research-based organizations throughout the world. An example is the company's alliance with Millennium Pharmaceuticals, Inc., in the field of genomics research. The initial focus of the alliance targets the development of new treatments for atherosclerosis, a leading cause of death in most Western societies. Lilly also has several global alliances with a focus on improving its manufacturing and marketing positions in key markets worldwide. For example, in China, the company has formed a joint venture with two Chinese organizations to build a multimillion-dollar pharmaceutical plant in Suzhou. Eli Lilly also has an agreement with Chugai Pharmaceuticals Co., Ltd., to co-develop and co-market Raloxifene in Japan, which is a new compound for treatment of osteoporosis.

The key trends affecting the pharmaceutical industry are protection of intellectual property, regulation, use of technology in drug discovery, and pressures for containing costs. The pharmaceutical industry is dependent upon effective protection of intellectual property rights, including patent protection for pharmaceutical products, which grants the developer of a new product an exclusive, yet limited, period in which to develop and market the product. Without this protection, pharmaceutical research companies would not be able to recoup the average investment of $350 to $400 million spent to discover and develop each new drug. There is a global effort to harmonize intellectual property through international trade agreements that facilitate implementation of effective patent protection for pharmaceutical products in markets that formerly provided inadequate protection. Regulation is another key trend affecting the industry. The current regulatory process has not kept pace with the technological advances of the pharmaceutical industry. For example, it takes approximately 15 years, on average, to approve a new drug: this is nearly six years longer than the average rate in the late 1960s. The pharmaceutical companies are working to reduce the time spent in the approval process.

Currently in the United States, approximately 15 percent of Gross Domestic Product (GDP) is spent on healthcare. As a result, there is increasing pressure to contain overall healthcare costs. Technology continues to be a key enabler of drug discovery and development. New technologies in the areas of genomics, combinatorial chemistry, molecular biology, and informatics facilitate better understanding of complex disease processes and aid in the development of new therapeutic approaches of preventing, treating, and curing diseases. There is also a marked increase in the number of strategic alliances that firms in this industry have developed with academic research institutions and biotechnology firms to speed up the application of new technologies in the drug discovery process. Finally, macro-trends such as aging populations, increased public expectations of the healthcare industry, and the need to reduce budget deficits have led to an increased pressure on pharmaceutical companies to contain rising healthcare costs. The traditional approach of controlling costs of each treatment element ignores the fact that limitations on one element may lead to increased patient morbidity and/or mortality, with a resulting increase in total healthcare costs. Therefore, certain leading-edge pharmaceutical firms such as Eli Lilly have used information technology and expertise in disease management to integrate all the participants in the healthcare chain; physicians, pharmacists, payers, providers, and patients. This integrated approach offers the potential for the best healthcare at an affordable cost.

DRIVERS OF ENVIRONMENTAL MANAGEMENT

Two important drivers characterize the company's emphasis on environmental issues: a need to develop a positive environment-oriented reputation and compliance with federal regulations. As an example of their desire to create a positive environmental image, it may be noted that the company participates in an environmental program called "Responsible Core," which was started by the Chemical Manufacturers Association (CMA). Other members of this association include DuPont and Dow. A company has to bid to obtain entry into this association, and membership in this organization connotes a commitment to environment issues. Similarly, a desire to create a positive image with the FDA can be seen from the company's effort to operate in accordance with "good manufacturing practices" as certified by the FDA. In addition, compliance with regulations of federal agencies is important.

The company believes in a "womb-to-tomb" philosophy for environmental management that spans the entire supply chain. For example, a solvent like acetone is shipped from suppliers in rail cars or trucks (or barges to an unloading dock). Being part of the association implies that suppliers must ship according to the Responsible Care (RC) philosophy. Similarly, suppliers are also encouraged to subscribe to RC philosophy because any potential liabilities arising out of the supplier's operations may render the buyer also liable. The product connectedness in the supply chain can be appreciated due to the fact that most pharmaceutical products are processed in two stages, bulk manufacturing or preparation of the active ingredient, and pharmaceutical manufacturing or putting the active ingredient in a pill or medication.

ENVIRONMENTAL POLICY

The mission of the company requires that all its facilities worldwide operate in a manner that protects human health and minimizes the impact of its operations on the environment. To carry out this mission, the company formulated an environmental policy with the following goals and objectives:

- To provide ongoing education and training for employees to effectively deal with day-to-day environmental responsibilities as well as environmental emergencies

- To comply with and exceed requirements of all applicable environment-related laws and regulations

- To adopt its own environmental quality standards in cases where existing laws and regulations are not adequate

- To make environmental considerations a priority throughout the process of developing new products

- To encourage and expect each employee to be environmentally responsible

- To encourage and promote waste minimization, the sustainable use of natural resources, recycling, energy efficiency, resource conservation, and resource recovery

- To communicate its commitment to environmental quality to its employees, shareholders, suppliers, customers, and the communities in which it operates

- To recognize and respond to the community's questions about its operations

- To actively participate with government agencies and other appropriate groups to ensure that the development and implementation of environmental policies, laws, regulations, and practices serve the public interest and are based on sound scientific judgment

- To regularly assess and report to management and the board of directors on the status of its compliance with this policy and with environmental laws and regulations

ENVIRONMENTAL PRACTICES

Global Sourcing

Global sourcing is another issue to be considered in environmental supply chain management. Eli Lilly has a global commodities manager who is part of the new product sourcing group for specialty chemicals and is responsible for procurement for six different bulk chemical manufacturing plants around the world. The resulting dilemma is how to formulate a guiding principle on environment-responsible sourcing that is applicable to suppliers worldwide. For this purpose, the company has a supplier selection questionnaire that contains items relating to technical and financial strength, quality systems and environment capability. An electronic profile on each supplier is maintained. A particularly thorny issue that the company faces is when it deals with "emerging-market suppliers." As the product matures in the market of developed countries and generics start to establish their presence, companies are forced to reduce cost to stay profitable. In order to achieve this objective, companies must tap the low-cost sourcing potential of emerging-market suppliers. Normally, these suppliers are not tapped during the front end of the product development process because federal agencies such as the FDA look at technical capabilities while approving new drug applications. Even on an administrative front, resorting to emerging-market suppliers may prove burdensome because the FDA might require a drug master file to be maintained by every supplier or may even require an audit of the supplier. If the suppliers do not pass the audit, then they become a source of supply disruption risk. This aspect is particularly relevant in the case of custom chemicals wherein cost differentials are typically higher. Also, due to the nature of custom chemicals, "latent impurities" do not show up until late in the manufacturing process resulting in considerable environment-related risks. The changes in healthcare environment are causing companies like Eli Lilly to put pressure on suppliers to decrease costs. In Germany and in the United Kingdom, custom chemical manufacturers are applying cost-reduction pressures on their first-tier suppliers, who are in turn resorting to emerging-market suppliers for less sophisticated products. A direct sourcing strategy results in a different set of risks.

Life-Cycle Analysis

"Speed to market" is a critical competitive priority for Eli Lilly, which does not believe in jeopardizing any effort that can contribute to the achievement of this goal. Consequently, the company ensures that suppliers conform to quality and environment standards. Any process change made by suppliers will have to be approved by the company, which is looking for safe, environment responsible processes.

It takes an average of 10 years for the company to develop and successfully introduce new products. To facilitate this process, early sourcing involvement is practiced. Other practices include environmental audits and total cost analysis. The product development group conducts life-cycle analyses to answer questions such as:

- What is the best route to manufacture a product?
- What are the safety issues inherent in the manufacture of the product?
- What is the capacity of suppliers to supply materials, and to treat compounds and effluents?

Sourcing decisions are affected by these considerations. For example, suppose that Compound X is manufactured in Process A. If an alternative process is proposed for the manufacture of Compound X, then new sourcing strategies and identification of global suppliers must be done.

Environmental Audits of Suppliers

Environmental performance is a prerequisite for supplier selection. Before selecting suppliers who manufacture heavy chemicals, specialty chemicals or commodity chemicals, a team of quality assurance executives from environmental affairs and purchasing organize and conduct a supplier environmental audit. The corporate environment group in Eli Lilly is a lean group in which the purchasing personnel are selected on the basis of knowledge of environmental issues. The purchasing personnel conduct supplier evaluations using five or six criteria to classify suppliers according to risk and then develop an audit schedule for suppliers. This implies a lot of responsibility for purchasing staff and a need for developing expertise via technical training.

Suppliers of Eli Lilly possess certifications such as ISO 9002 and ISO 14000, which make them uniquely valuable in terms of the skills and qualifications required for manufacturing fine chemicals. All new suppliers are audited, especially in cases of repeat purchases.

Environmental Performance Measurement

The company is a strong advocate of the "environmental value-added" (EVA) concept. This concept forces a systematic evaluation of allocation of scarce assets. Traditionally, the company had a high degree of vertical integration that created a lot of waste, thereby creating a need for waste treatment facilities. Under the new EVA philosophy, most of the manufacturing activities are outsourced to suppliers. Antibiotics are very expensive to produce, and investment in waste treatment assets has to be recouped by the main product. However, new products are not as asset intensive. Under EVA, suppliers do basic developmental work for the company. For example,

Eastman Chemicals, Kingspot, Tennessee is a supplier of solvents and performs the synthesis of compounds. Then chemists from both companies work together to optimize value along the supply chain. The company solves the make-buy decision by identifying the most productive source of value creation that results in assets that maximize EVA. This decision is made by a team, which includes financial analysts.

Environmentally based actions end up as excellent business decisions. The market usually rewards "innovation delivered quickly." However, innovations may hinder environmental posture and efficient cost-competitive manufacturing. In such situations, it may be argued that getting to market first and then retrofitting manufacturing processes to reduce waste may be a desirable business choice.

Environmental Risk Analysis

For a typical antibiotic product, the company buys approximately 100 different chemicals. Purchasing is closely involved in process design by working with development chemists and suggesting sources for chemicals. The company has a capability to recover solvents after use in the manufacturing process. The solvents can be resold to another manufacturer or distributor. The company typically examines the risks of product liability in deciding whether to sell the recovered solvent to another manufacturer or distributor. Another relevant issue in this decision is the cleaning of the solvent. In the original manufacturing process, solvents such as acetone are used to wash the centrifuges. The process waste obtained when the filtrate is collected cannot be used for any useful purpose. Therefore, in the future environmental management system, the company requires the supplier to collect and clean the filtrate and then reship the solvent to the company as part of their commitment to environmental responsibility.

The company conducts a systematic risk analysis that includes an assessment of biological risks and liability risks. The lowering of risks has to be evaluated from a customer's value point of view. A customer who is sick merely seeks the drug and does not care about the sustainability effect on the company. The evaluation of risk as far as suppliers are concerned is based on plant, process, technical capability, and financial resources. Based on this assessment, purchasing is advised regarding supplier selection, and possible regulatory and operational liabilities.

LESSONS LEARNED

Eli Lilly's case description suggests the following key success factors to be critical for successful environmental management:

- An initial strategy of speed to market followed by incremental changes in process designs that are environmentally friendly is important.

- A supply chain emphasis is required for optimizing environment value added (EVA) performance.

- The ability to recover solvents after use in the manufacturing processes is critical.

- An ability to tap emerging-market suppliers for less sophisticated products and manage associative risks is important.

- A lean corporate environment group is desirable for expediting decision-making.

This case study also has several implications for environmental supply chain management as listed below:

- Safe and environmentally responsible processes are important criteria for supplier selection.

- Supplier audits on environmental issues require a cross-functional initiative involving employees from quality assurance, environmental affairs, and purchasing. Similarly, teams should include financial analysts who decide whether suppliers will be the most productive from the perspective of maximizing EVA make make-or-buy decisions.

- Adherence of suppliers to quality and environment standards is a necessary prerequisite for achieving a company's objective of speed to market.

- Because of the long lead times for new products (10 years), companies need to resort to early sourcing and early supplier involvement in basic product developmental work.

- Sourcing decisions take into consideration safety issues, capacity of suppliers, and ability to treat compounds and effluents.

- Because of an emphasis on a lean group, purchasing has more responsibility to conduct timely supplier evaluations using criteria such as risk and environmental capability. This in turn affects the training and technical expertise expected of purchasing staff.

- Because of the emphasis on environmental value-added performance, companies turn to suppliers for use of their waste treatment facilities. Companies also seek to develop suppliers who can collect, clean and reship processed waste back to the company.

- The range of influence for sourcing strategies and supplier identification is global.

GRUNDFOS

COMPANY BACKGROUND

The Grundfos Group is well known throughout the world for high-quality pumps and pumping systems. Their pumps bring fresh drinking water to torrid desert regions, circulate warm water in colder climates, transport water in slaughterhouses in Europe and oil rigs in the Far East. They irrigate tulip fields in Holland and fruit and vegetable farms in California and Australia. The company is known around the world for its reliability, credibility, and innovation.

Since its founding, the company has always tried to manage and control, as far as possible, pump development and production, from the initial processing of the raw materials to the finished product. Its drive for superior quality covers the whole production chain, from product development to the final sale, and is demonstrated by becoming the world's first pump manufacturer to receive the ISO 9001 Quality Certificate in 1989. Today, Grundfos companies operate in Germany, England, France, the United States, Taiwan, and Australia.

Grundfos demonstrates a high degree of environmental consciousness by concentrating on improvements in its internal working environment and by minimizing the impacts on the external environment. As early as 1992, Grundfos was one of the first Danish enterprises to sign the ICC Environmental Charter, the declaration of trade and industry on sustainable development.

The company's products comprise a wide variety of groundwater pumping systems, domestic water supply pumps, and circulator pumps for heating and air-conditioning systems. The company is currently in the process of unleashing a wave of new product by tapping into three new technologies of stainless powder metal, permanent magnets, and thermally sprayed coatings. The advantage of powder metal is that the process enables the pressing of geometrically complicated details with a high degree of raw material utilization. The permanent magnets that can be used in electrical devices, magnetic bearings, and couplings considerably improve the strength and tightness of the finished products. With regard to the environment, magnets have the advantage of re-use without any environmental consequences. Thermally sprayed coatings are used in applications that demand a high degree of abrasion-resistance, hardness, and/or corrosion resistance. The technology is particularly suitable for mass production and has the advantage of rendering even soft materials abrasion resistant in crucial wearing areas. Common among the three technologies are the benefits of producing stronger, more durable, and cheaper goods than corresponding products produced with other technologies.

At the close of the 1997 financial year, the company posted a 15.5 percent increase in sales turnover at DKK 6,682 million, and profit before tax increased from DKK 364 million to DKK 421 million. The number of employees in the group has gone up from 8,805 to 9,154. In 1996-97, Grundfos manufactured more than eight million pumps to take an increasing share of the world demand, most notably in Eastern Europe. With an increase in research and development activities of 11.1 percent relative to the previous accounting year, Grundfos spent a total of DKK 289 million on direct product development. The company has set an ambitious plan to achieve a consolidated turnover of DKK 10 billion by the end of the year 2000. It hopes to make a strong presence in the expanding markets of Eastern Europe, China, India and South America.

ENVIRONMENTAL POSTURE OF THE COMPANY

Grundfos attaches great importance to the environment with a pervasive emphasis on the theme of sustainability in all operations. In 1996, the company's largest production plant in Denmark was granted the Environment Certificate under the ISO 14001 standard and also gained approval under EMAS, the new European certification standard. Grundfos strives to achieve 100 percent recycling of the materials from old Grundfos pumps. In the future, the company wants all its production companies worldwide to apply for environmental certification.

ENVIRONMENTAL PRACTICES

On behalf of its customers, the company conducts a life-cycle analysis of all new products with a view to ensuring that no unnecessary materials are used in their manufacture and that they do not consume unnecessary energy. This is a direct response to requirements of customers who are paying more and more attention to the materials that have gone into products and the consequences of their installation for the environment. One facilitating tool for LCA is environmental mapping that includes a comprehensive tracing of all manufacturing activities and asks questions such as:

- What do our 403 chimneys emit into the atmosphere?
- How much electricity, heat, fuel, and water are consumed?
- How much raw materials are consumed?

On the basis of responses to these types of questions, targets for future consumption of resources are set. This practice has resulted in benefits in multiple areas. For instance, in a recent year, consumption of electricity was reduced by 20 percent, water by 6 percent, and heating by 10 percent.

At an early stage in the development process Grundfos ensures an environmental assessment of all new products. Life-cycle assessments are performed to give an overview of the products' environmental "cradle to grave" impact. The results of the LCA—energy consumption, material selection, disposal, etc.—are assessed with a view to further optimization. LCAs of the company's products show that over 95 percent of the product life-cycle impact on the environment typically derives from the production of energy for the operating stage. Due to this fact, top priority is given to energy utilization when developing new products.

Environmental Auditing

The company has a comprehensive audit program that includes all the activities carried out on all locations. The internal audit takes place once a year in each division. External auditors in liaison with specialists of the trade carry out these audits. All audit results are reported to the management of the division concerned. Once a year, top management performs an evaluation of the entire environmental management system and decides whether the system adequately complies with both legislative requirements and the company's targets, and the targets for the upcoming period.

ENVIRONMENTAL ORGANIZATION

The environmental organization structure is designed to ensure compliance with legislative requirements as well as continual environmental improvements in all functions within the group. The environmental and quality manager is responsible for the compliance of environmental management procedures. The individual functional managers are responsible for the environmental impacts from their fields of responsibility and for providing adequate training for employees within their area. The works managers are locally responsible for the production within the facilities. To ensure adequate know-how in relation to day-to-day environmental activities the company, in liaison with the trade committee of Danish metal industries (Metalindustriens Brancheudvalg), has developed courses specifically designed to promote environmental effectiveness.

HOECHST AG

COMPANY BACKGROUND

Hoechst is the world's largest manufacturer of chemical products (see Figure 18 for Hoechst sales and operating profit status for 1995). Despite substantial downsizing in recent years, Hoechst remains one of Europe's 10 largest employers. Two factors are changing the role of basic suppliers, such as Hoechst, of essential inputs for the industrial process. One factor is the globalization of the world economy and the second factor is the decreasing importance of economies of scale.

Globalization has created many capable new market entrants in a variety of emerging countries both as producers and consumers of basic inputs. Economies of scale are no longer as important as they once were, with smaller manufacturing units able to produce some products more efficiently and respond more flexibly to changing market conditions than can their larger counterparts.

These market forces have freed many consumers of basic chemical products from traditional geographical constraints and have allowed them to shop from a variety of companies. If necessary, these same consumers have been able to move production closer to essential and efficient suppliers.

The current environment has also given some competitive advantages to smaller chemical firms that can respond more flexibly to special needs and that can integrate the benefits of new technology more quickly. At the same time, more active investors are looking for higher rates of return than smaller companies are often able to provide.

Hoechst has focused on increasing shareholder value by operating globally, increasing the responsibility and authority of its strategic business units, and building up strategic business units of its organization that can respond rapidly to technological change.

DIRECTIONS

Hoechst has focused on increasing the value of the firm to shareholders. This has involved decentralization of the strategic business units, selling shares in each component industry, carving out a major role in biotechnology, and conducting an active Asian strategy (see Figure 19 for a graph of Hoechst Assets by Business Area). Within the past year, Hoechst has taken the following steps:

1. Hoechst has substantially altered its organization of internal management by moving to a holding company structure in which the board operates as a portfolio manager providing

FIGURE 18

SALES AND OPERATING PROFIT BY DIVISION AND AFFILIATE IN DM MILLIONS

	Sales	Operating Profit	Return (%)
Pharmaceuticals	11,530	532	4.6
Diagnostics	799	-14	-1.8
AgrEvo	3,041	147	4.8
Hoechst Rousell Vet	711	65	9.1
Basic Chemicals	5,391	1,166	21.6
Specialty Chemicals	8,160	274	3.4
Fibers	7,195	521	7.2
Plastics	3,603	352	9.8
Technical Polymers	1,441	-80	-5.6
Messers Griesheim	2,290	238	10.4
Herberts	2,151	74	3.4
SGL Carbon	1,549	265	17.1
Other Activities	4,316	51	1.2
Totals	**52,177**	**3,591**	**6.9**

strategic direction and support for the firm as a whole but giving its major business units; basic chemicals, polyester, pharmaceuticals, animal health, technical polymers, and specialty chemicals; independent profit and loss responsibilities.

2. Hoechst is prepared to value each of its strategic business units individually and issue public shares separately.

3. Hoechst has identified the life sciences group as the strategic future growth unit and aggressively applied biotechnology to crop protection. Hoechst intends to move from protecting crops to improving resistance, quality, and yield of crops. To further this strategy, Hoechst purchased Plant General Systems, one of Europe's largest biotechnology firms.

4. Hoechst has identified Asia as a prime growth area, establishing goals for raising its share of sales in Asia from less than 10 percent today to 20 percent within 10 years on investments and 10 percent per year growth rates in revenues. Hoechst plans to invest $1 billion in China to become the largest chemical company operating in that country (see Figure 20 for a depiction of Hoechst Assets Region).

FIGURE 19
HOECHST ASSETS BY BUSINESS AREA

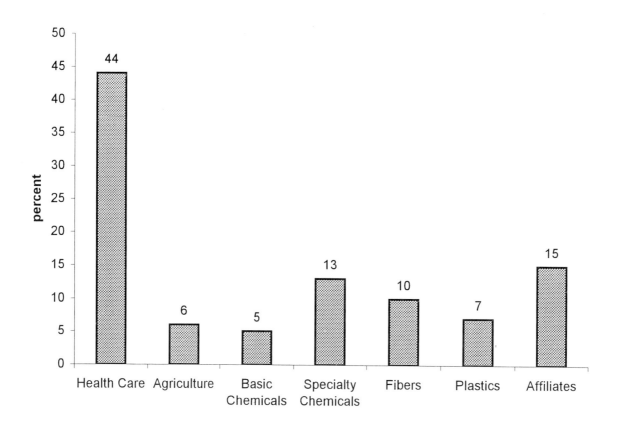

ENVIRONMENTAL PROTECTION AND SAFETY

Hoechst continues to make good progress in environmental protection by reducing emissions from their facilities by investing in sophisticated process technology and strategically focusing their product range. At the same time, end-of-pipe environmental protection for the treatment of exhaust air and wastewater as well as waste disposal is becoming less necessary (see Figures 21 through 23 for an approximation of Hoechst Air Emissions, Hoechst Waste Quantities, and Hoechst Residual Wastewater Pollution, respectively, over the last 10 years). Over the last 10 years Hoechst production output increased substantially. Environmentally related operating costs in 1995 amounted to DM 1.5 billion, 4 percent less than in the previous year. A further DM 265 million was invested in environmental protection plant and equipment.

At the Griesheim and Hoechst plant sites two accidents occurred at the end of January 1996 that drew strong public criticism because Hoechst was slow to report them. Hoechst reacted to this criticism by immediately appointing emergency managers for all German sites. These individuals, who work in addition to existing safety organizations, are responsible for implementing the necessary communication measures in the event of an accident. In addition to the measures resolved in previous years, Hoechst earmarked a further DM 150 million for the inspection and modernization of the control and measurement technology at these two locations.

In 1995, Hoechst started integrating the management systems for quality, plant safety, environmental protection, and occupational health and safety at their site in Frankfurt. The various sectors are no longer being viewed in isolation. Instead, elements such as regulations and audits, information, and documentation systems are being combined. A uniform documentation and auditing system will not only make their organization more efficient and transparent to everyone involved, but will also promote an exchange of knowledge at the same time.

FIGURE 20

HOECHST ASSETS BY REGION

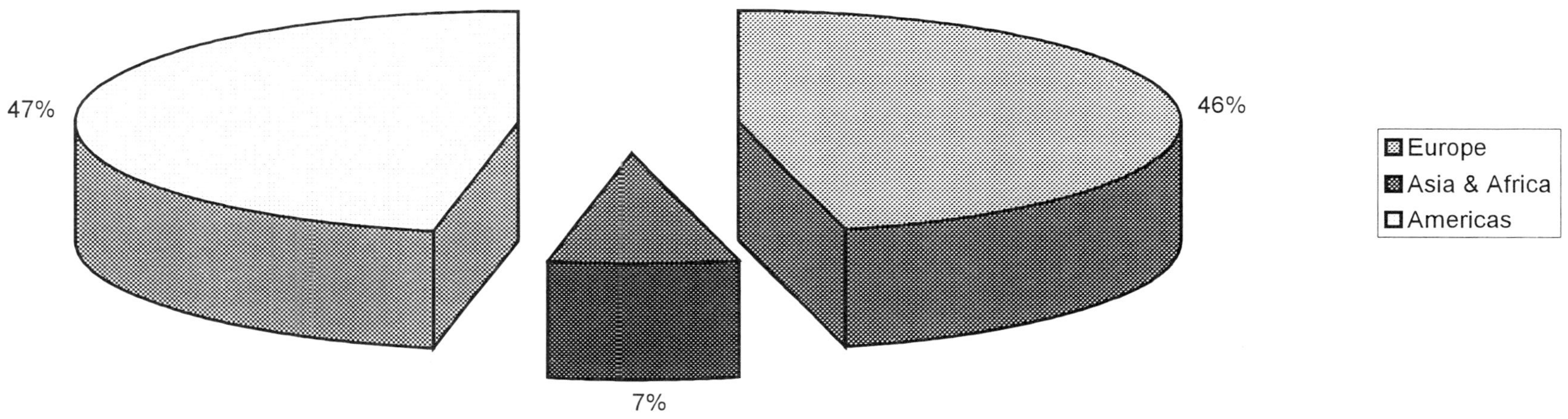

46%

7%

47%

Europe
Asia & Africa
Americas

FIGURE 21

HOECHST AIR EMISSIONS

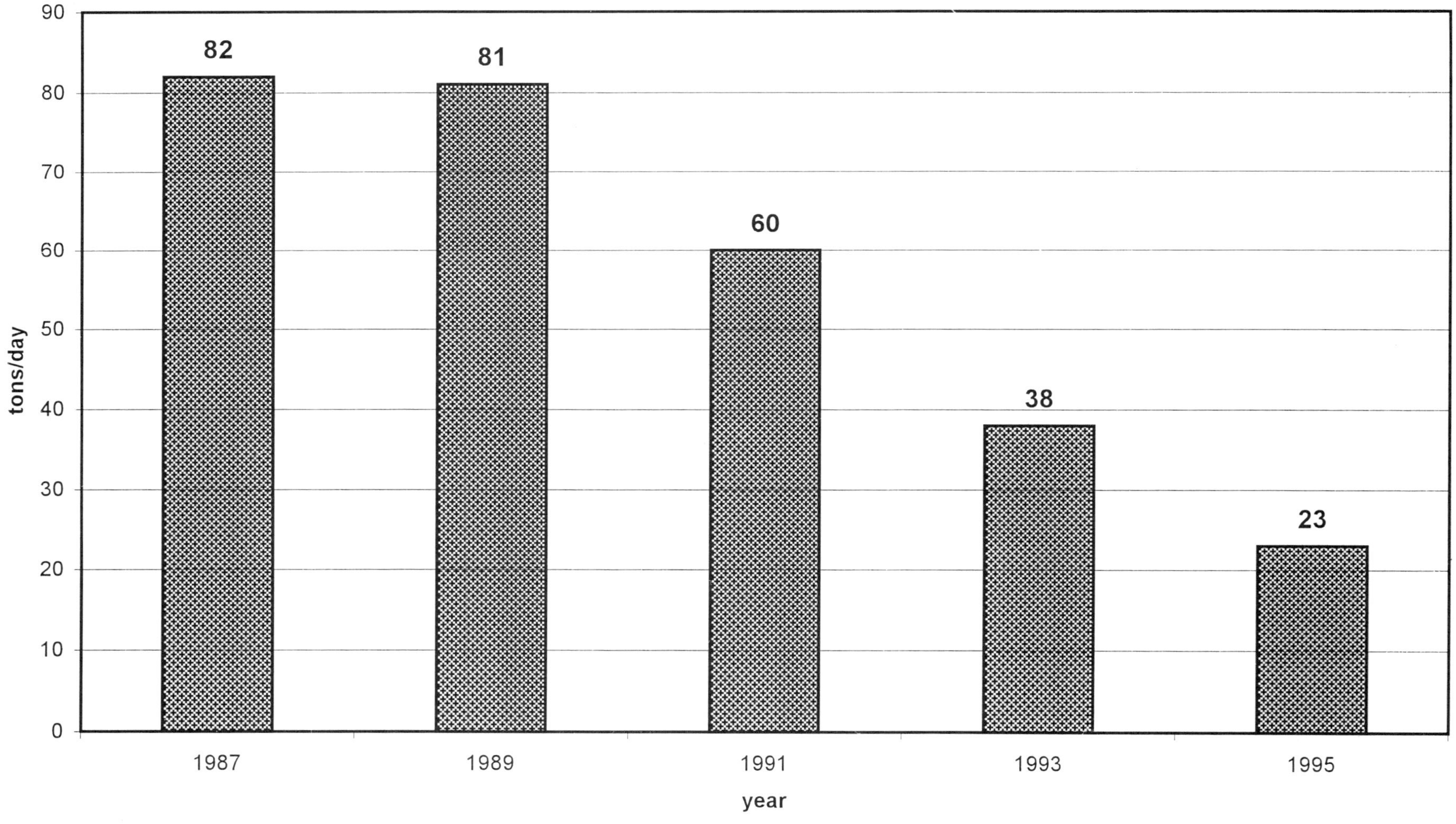

FIGURE 22
HOECHST WASTE QUANTITIES

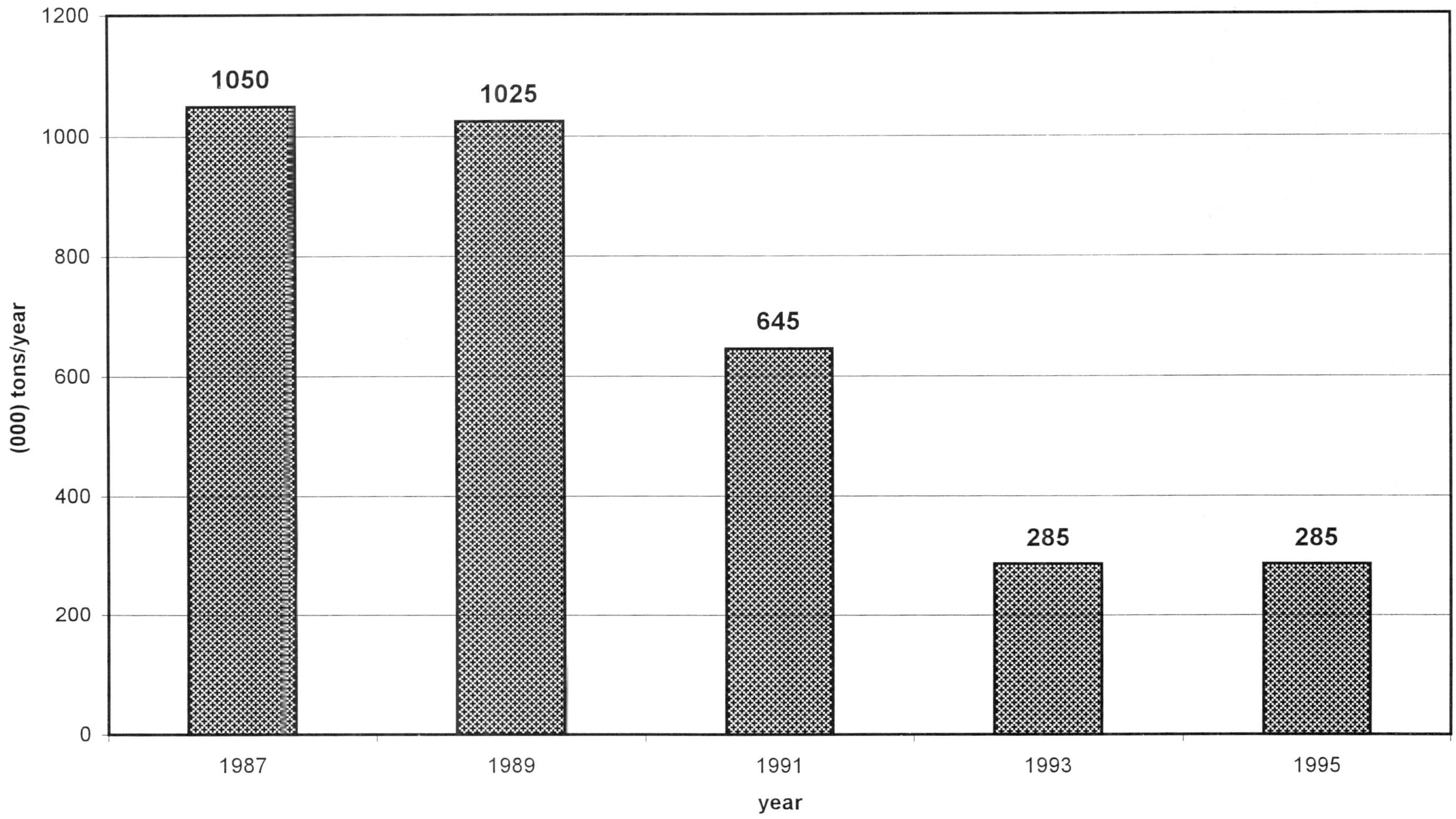

61

FIGURE 23

HOECHST RESIDUAL WASTEWATER POLLUTION

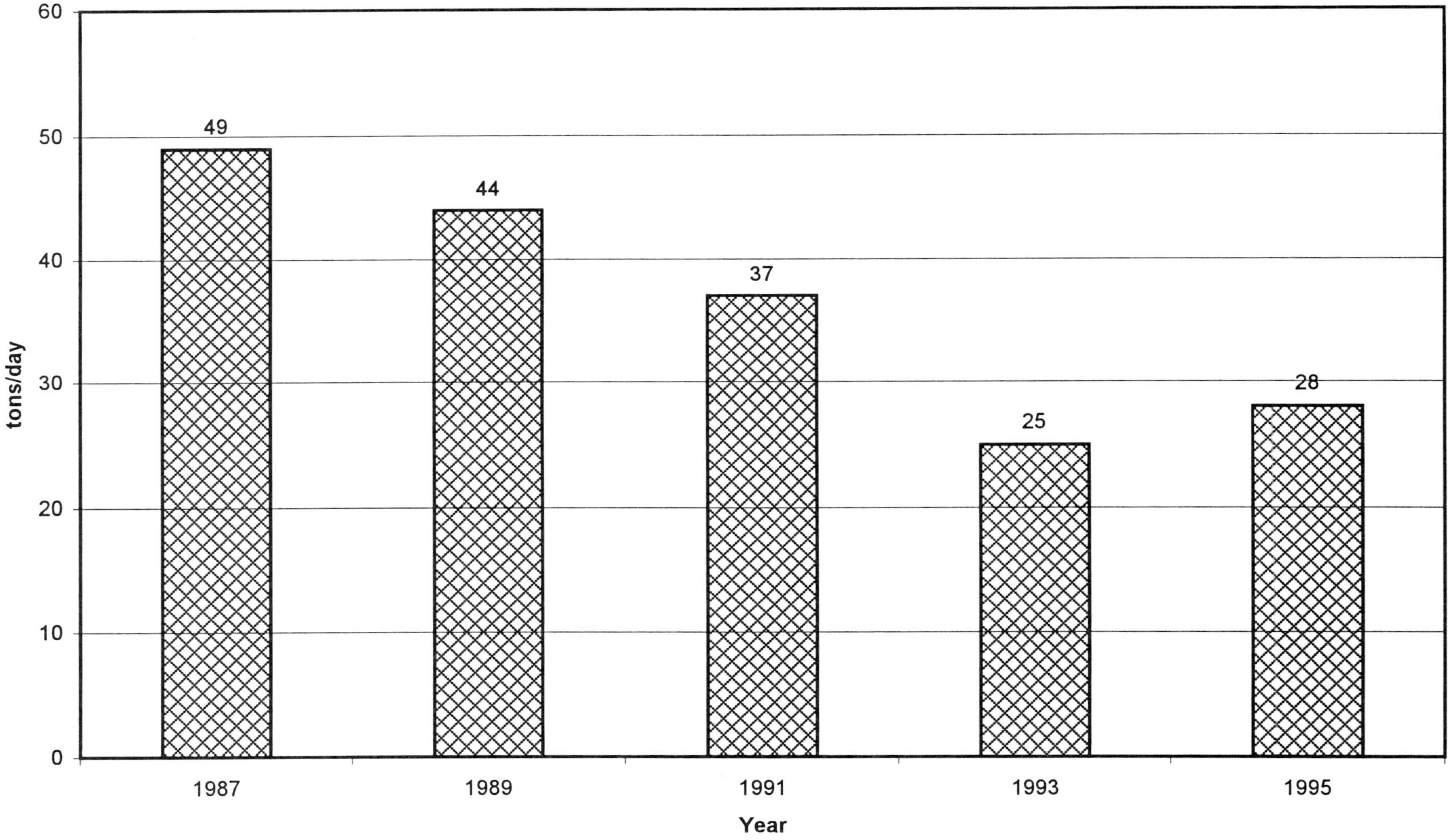

UNIFORM ENVIRONMENTAL PROTECTION STANDARDS WORLDWIDE

In the fall of 1995, the Bad Hersfeld site of Hoechst became the first chemical industry facility in Germany to gain certification under the EU's environmental management and auditing scheme (EMAS). All sites in Europe are due to be audited by the year 2000. Hoechst will also be playing an active part in development of the ISO standard series 14000, which will pave the way for the worldwide introduction of comparable environmental management systems.

The different procedures used to record and assess substances are being combined in a new system. In the future, all starting, intermediate, and end products will be evaluated against uniform environment and health criteria. The assessments will be transferred to a global product information database.

Hoechst is participating in a European pilot project aimed at avoiding the risks that arise from the landfilling of residues commonly produced by the chemical industry. In the future, Hoechst's residues will be landfilled only after being rendered inert and/or mineralized by incineration, for example.

SAFETY AS AN OBLIGATION

Hoechst uses a variety of methods to ensure global compliance with their safety standards. They include routine safety audits, the constant monitoring of production processes, and the continual inspection of plants. They also appraise and advise on capital projects and process changes, and they provide ongoing training of safety personnel. Regional safety conferences are also held. The transport of hazardous materials is a major concern for Hoechst; however, logistics systems effectively support safety in this area. Specific safety precautions such as checks on incoming and outgoing shipments at all sites reduce the risks to employees, local residents, and the environment.

LESSONS LEARNED

- The realities of international competition mandate that Hoechst must buy a substantive amount of product from "dirty" production sites worldwide. This has placed a great deal of responsibility with the global sourcing organization to know the environmental regulations worldwide and to work closely with global suppliers to effectively manage their processes for environmental effectiveness.

- Hoechst has discovered that the investment in new technology can both reduce environmentally hazardous emissions as well as reduce cost through increasingly efficient production. Simply, environmental effectiveness and cost efficiency correlate well together.

- As cost pressures continue to intensify, the linkages between technological improvements, cost containment, and environmental effectiveness will only grow in importance.

HONDA OF AMERICA MANUFACTURING

COMPANY BACKGROUND

Crossing the Pacific in 1959 with its revolutionary Super Cub motorbike, Honda first came ashore in the Americas more than 35 years ago. Before long, the slogan "you meet the nicest people on a Honda" became a household phrase, and Honda was on its way to becoming a firmly established presence in the North American market with an extensive sales network.

In 1972, the Honda Civic hit the marketplace with the revolutionary CVCC clean engine, which provided the foundation for every Honda automobile that has been manufactured since. In 1976, Honda opened a motorcycle factory in Brazil, created under the principle of "taking manufacturing to our markets." This was followed in 1979 by domestic production at the Ohio motorcycle plant, and in 1982 with passenger car production, the first such venture in America by any Japanese automaker. Canada became home to a Honda automobile manufacturing facility in 1986.

Honda in America has been a pioneer in creating corporate entities that grow and flourish in their own markets under their own initiative, and make valuable contributions as an integral part of the local business community.

CORPORATE PROFILE

Established 48 years ago, Honda Motor Co., Ltd., is one of today's leading manufacturers of automobiles and the largest manufacturer of motorcycles in the world. The company is recognized internationally for its expertise and leadership in developing and manufacturing a wide variety of products ranging from small general purpose engines to specialty sports cars that incorporate Honda's highly efficient internal combustion engine technology. Over nine million Honda engines were produced worldwide during the fiscal year ending March 31, 1996.

By following a corporate policy that emphasizes originality, innovation, and efficiency in every facet of its operations, from product development and manufacturing to marketing, Honda has striven to attain its goal of customer satisfaction. Through a worldwide commitment to advancing this goal, Honda and its many partners who share in this commitment have succeeded in creating a global network with 89 production facilities in 33 countries that supply Honda products to most countries in the world.

ENVIRONMENTAL ISSUES AT HONDA

A major goal of Honda, and one that has been successfully implemented, is to be "world class" in environmental issues. From a purchasing point of view, Honda strives to set an environmental example for their suppliers. This environmental sensitivity is based on a long-standing corporate philosophy that is stressed to the heart of the company. For example, the eight members on the board of directors, three of whom are from procurement backgrounds, apply four criteria to each potential decision:

1. How will this decision affect our associates?

2. How will this decision affect our suppliers?

3. How will this decision impact our environment?

4. How will this decision affect our stockholders?

At Honda, the purchasing function is considered a major component of corporate strategy, in general and environmental strategy, in particular. Much of this prominence is due to the fact that nearly 80 percent of the costs of a new vehicle is comprised of purchased goods and services. Clearly, the role played by suppliers is critical to Honda's success.

The organization structure at Honda reflects the importance placed on purchasing decisions. A senior vice-president who reports directly to the president of American Honda heads the supply chain management group, formerly known as purchasing. This is the same organization structure as for engineering, another critical component of Honda strategy.

Honda views environmental sensitivity as a marketing strategy. Honda sees the need to continually strengthen their environmental image in the eyes of the consumer. Strategically, Honda wants to be viewed as first on environmental issues. For example, the CVCC engine, the core of Honda production expertise, meets all federal and state-mandated air quality emission standards without the use of a catalytic converter. This is one example of the use of environmental technology actually reducing costs. As another example, the President of Honda Motor Company has mandated that the various corporate groups implement ISO 14000 standards promptly.

A key component for implementing Honda's environmental policies has been a close working relationship between the supply chain management (SCM) group and engineering. Note that Honda views itself as an engine manufacturer and sells automobiles and motorcycles in order to sell engines. Environmental effectiveness as it relates to manufacturing engines manifests itself during the design stage of the product lifecycle, where the "rubber meets the road." In order to maintain the constant advancement of technology, Honda has implemented a policy to continually fund research and development on a steady basis. A key component of this desire was moving research and development funding away from being sensitive to the inevitable business cycles. Honda had tied research and development funding to a constant percentage of gross sales, which has steadily increased over the years.

The research and development/purchasing linkage is critical to many Honda initiatives, including environmental sensitivity and is fostered organizationally. For example, an entire segment of research and development employees was physically moved to a section close to the SCM group to maximize interaction. In a similar vein, purchasing has 13 designated liaisons that coordinate the interface between suppliers and the engineering groups.

The relationship between the supply base and Honda was not always so fluid. Prior to three years ago it was very difficult to get any supplier-initiated changes through the process. Because of the potential cost impact, suppliers were then brought in to get value analysis suggestions in all areas. This move resulted in many cost savings and culminated in the 1998 Honda Accord; 500 supplier-suggested improvements resulted in 200 changes being made in the automobile's design and thus reduced expected costs of manufacturing the vehicle by 20 percent. Presently, life-cycle cost analyses for environmental suggestions are not used, but Honda is moving quickly to develop a method of life-cycle analysis that will cut across part and service costing areas.

The SCM group does not consider environmental issues as part of the supplier certification process. However, it does keep a constant eye on supplier environmental management policies so that any negative supplier publicity does not turn into bad publicity for Honda.

Today, Honda views its future as inextricably tied to supplier expertise in many areas. A great deal of concurrent engineering is performed with suppliers, and its importance is growing rapidly. Honda has found that the best place to implement changes that will reap environmental savings is during the early design stage where, possibly more than in other areas, environmental savings must be "designed into" the finished product.

NOVARTIS (FORMERLY CIBA-GEIGY)

COMPANY BACKGROUND

In April 1996, the shareholders of Sandoz and Ciba-Geigy agreed to the merger of the two Basel-based Swiss enterprises to form a new company called Novartis. This was the largest corporate merger in history. Prior to the merger, the combined worldwide sales of Ciba-Geigy and Sandoz were approximately 36 billion Swiss francs and the combined research and development expenditures were 3 billion Swiss francs. The merger brought Novartis leadership positions in the life sciences, genetics, and crop protection strategic business units. It now holds second position in pharmaceuticals, optics, seeds, animal health, and nutrition businesses. It also holds fifth position and seventh positions in ophthalmic and consumer health sectors.

The name "Novartis" comes from the Latin term *novae artes* or new arts and new skills. Through this name, the company seeks to communicate a mission of utilizing scientific research, imagination, and new technology to provide ever-greater benefits for humankind. With an annual investment in research and development of approximately 3.5 billion Swiss francs, the company is committed to developing tomorrow's life science solutions. Headquartered in Basel, Switzerland, Novartis employs approximately 90,000 people in more than 100 countries around the world. The company's strategic focus on life sciences led to the divestment of the Specialty Chemicals Division of Ciba and the Construction Chemicals Division of Sandoz. The company aspires to capture and hold a leadership position in their healthcare, agriculture, and nutrition businesses with a strong, sustainable performance based on continuous innovation.

The company has a strategy of investing in emerging technology, such as gene therapy. Its in-house and external efforts span diverse research strategies, including ex-vivo and in-vivo applications and viral/non-viral vector systems. It has major alliances with reputable pharmaceutical institutions such as Scripps Research Institute, Pharmacopeia, Johns Hopkins Consortium, Isis Pharmaceuticals, and the Max Planck Institute in Germany. It also has in-house research centers of excellence in Switzerland, the United States, United Kingdom, Austria, and Japan that are focused on the company's core therapeutic areas of expertise. In these centers, the most advanced technologies in bioinformatics, genomics, combinatorial chemistry, and high-throughput screening have been implemented.

The company's future strategy is to command global leadership in the life sciences sector with a sharp focus on three core businesses: healthcare, which comprises pharmaceuticals, consumer health, genetics and vision care; agribusiness, which comprises crop protection, seeds and animal health; and nutrition.

OPERATING HIGHLIGHTS

Novartis is a world leader in life sciences with core businesses in healthcare, agribusiness, and nutrition. In 1996, Novartis achieved group sales of 27.6 billion Swiss francs, of which 16.3 billion were in healthcare, 7.6 billion in agribusiness, and 3.7 billion in nutrition. The company also invested more than 3 billion Swiss francs in research and development. Operating income in 1996 increased by 25 percent to 4 billion Swiss francs, despite significant increases in investments in research and development (+18 percent) and marketing/distribution (+27 percent). The operating margin improved from 23 percent to 24.2 percent, primarily due to increased volumes, merger-related synergies, and a net devaluation of the Swiss franc against major currencies. Corporate overhead expenses were reduced by 128 million Swiss francs due to synergies from the merger.

In 1996, the healthcare division recorded above-average operating income growth of 7 percent to 3.9 billion Swiss francs. In agribusiness, operating income reached 1.4 billion Swiss francs, an increase of 5 percent. However, the operating income of the nutrition division was lower than in 1995, due mainly to expenses for launching new products, corrective measures caused by an increasingly competitive U.S. market environment, and stagnant industry growth in Europe.

ENVIRONMENTAL POSTURE OF THE COMPANY

In 1997, the company released its first consolidated annual report on health, safety, and environmental protection (HSE), which emphasized its philosophy — that every product and service provided by the company aims to combine economic benefits with better health, safety, and a better environment. In addition to providing presentations of the company's HSE approach and policies, the report highlights the progress achieved in the merger year and includes key performance figures. In their joint preface to the report, Chairman Alex Krauer and President Daniel Vasella emphasized the company policy of maintaining and continually improving performance in HSE and communicating openly the benefits and the potential risks of the company's products and activities.

In 1996 Novartis invested 230 million Swiss francs in HSE in addition to its operational HSE costs of more than a billion Swiss francs. The favorable trends in productivity and energy achieved in the recent past were sustained in 1996: production increased by 3 percent but there was a further decrease in the energy consumed. In line with this trend, carbon dioxide emissions, heavy-metal content in waste water, and emissions of nonhalogenated volatile organic compounds (VOCs) were reduced (VOC emissions are due to solvents used in production processes). Halogenated VOC emissions (at one site) and hazardous waste increased in line with production. There were no fatal accidents in manufacturing. In 1996, HSE audits were conducted at 64 sites and identified no serious problems.

Brief History of Environmental Management

The emphasis on environmental issues started as early as in 1960. Over a period of three decades the company has made significant progress in environmental issues, as can be seen from the brief history of environmental management in the company.

- 1960—Laboratory for testing chemicals for fire and explosion hazards established.

- 1970—Laboratory established for testing thermal safety of chemical reactions, for research on electrostatic ignition sources, and for development of measures against gas and dust explosions

- 1972—First full-time environmental officers appointed in Novartis' plants

- 1974—Executive Committee approves "Safety Principles" which include specific directives, guidelines and information on safety matters.

- 1978—Introduction of method of systematic risk analysis.

- 1980—Environmental and safety audit programs are introduced.

- 1984—Executive Committee approves "Principles for Environmental Protection in Production."

- 1985—First corporate seminars given on safety and environmental protection.

- 1987—First internal environmental report issued giving details of emissions from the different company sites.

- 1988—Executive Committee approves "Principles on Product Safety."

- 1990—Standardized reporting on Safety, Energy, and Environmental Protection (SEEP) is introduced for the company sites.

- 1991—Executive Committee approves new corporate "Energy Policy."

- 1992—Novartis becomes member of the Business Council for Sustainable Development.

- 1993—Richard Barth, CEO of Novartis-USA is named a member of President Clinton's Council on Sustainable Development. The first Corporate Environmental Report is issued.

- 1994—First independent assessment of SEEP environmental auditing system is conpleted.

- 1995—Novartis is awarded World Environmental Center's Gold Medal for International Corporate Environmental Achievement.

DRIVERS FOR ENVIRONMENTAL CONSCIOUSNESS

The drivers for being environmentally conscious were primarily external in nature arising from governmental regulations and market opportunities to tap the growing demand for environmentally compatible products.

NOVARTIS' ENVIRONMENTAL PRACTICES

Several environmental practices are used in the company. Benefit-risk analysis is conducted for core processes to ascertain the risks associated with manufacturing and distribution processes and their effect on the environment. This analysis is communicated widely within the company and is also disseminated as publicly available information. The company has explicit future-oriented goals relating to environmental performance called Vision 2000; this contains broad responsibilities and actions required for all employees for contributing to better environmental performance. This vision statement also contains quantitative targets for the different facets of environmental performance, such as, air pollution, waste generation and treatment, and energy consumption.

The company follows one uniform policy with respect to safety, health, and environment called an Integrated Environmental Management System. This system was adapted to correspond to the ISO 14001 environmental management standard. This was done for two reasons: if the company decides to seek ISO 14000 certification, it would be able to achieve this certification with minimal overhauling of operations, and it also wanted to benchmark environmental operations according to an internationally renowned standard, which would then facilitate better global operations and recognition.

The company has an external consulting agency conduct an environmental and safety audit of its operations to ensure objectivity, accuracy, and reliability. To prepare for this audit, the company has prepared a procedure manual that assigns clear responsibilities for the various activities needed to achieve environmental excellence in its operations. Specifically, the manual incorporates an objective measurement system called a Safety, Energy, and Environment Protection (SEEP), which allows the company to obtain real time, accurate information on more than 90 percent of emissions resulting from company operations worldwide. Another example of documentation relates to forms that capture life-cycle assessments to determine types of packaging that are most environmentally compatible.

Other environmentally sound practices include an employee competition to generate ideas of how to increase awareness of energy consumption and establish targets for energy management. The employee competition in its inception year generated almost 100 ideas for energy savings.

LESSONS LEARNED

The key lessons learned from this case study are summarized as follows:

- It is desirable to make early financial investment in environmental protection. Novartis was one of the first European companies to formulate environmental policies (1972).

- Top management commitment to environmental issues (as indicated by a higher position for environmental and safety department in the organization chart) is critical for success.

- Decentralization of environmental specialists in the different business units is most efficient.

- Environmental considerations should be viewed as an inseparable part of business performance. It is useful to set quantitative targets for different environmental performance measures.

NOVO NORDISK

COMPANY BACKGROUND

Novo Nordisk is based in Denmark with offices in 54 countries and major production plants in Denmark and the United States. The company has three strategic business units (SBUs): healthcare, healthcare discovery and development, and enzymes. It is the world's leading supplier of insulin and diabetes-care products. It is also the world's largest producer of industrial enzymes with a market share of approximately 50 percent. The company sells its products in more than 130 countries around the world. A majority of its sales (97 percent) come from foreign markets (i.e., outside Denmark). Overall sales in 1995 were DKK 13,723 million (1 percent increase from the previous year). Its biggest market is Japan, but the company is experiencing the highest sales growth in the United States (17 percent) followed by Japan (8 percent) and Germany (7 percent). Novo Nordisk employs approximately 13,000 employees of who around 3,000 are in research and development (23 percent). The company spends an average of 14 percent of its turnover on research and development; expenditures in 1995 were DKK 1,950 million. In 1995 alone, the company filed 308 new patent applications (the largest number in a single year in the company's history).

Novo Nordisk has major customer groups for enzyme business in a wide range of industries such as animal feed, food, brewing, detergent (largest segment), fats and oils, leather, personal care, protein, pulp and paper, starch and textile. The company faces intense competitive pressure for increasing productivity, flexibility, and innovation capability. Important trends affecting the company include the consolidation of the supply and customer base, an increased customer emphasis on cost and value, significantly shorter product development times, and intensifying global competition. The corporate strategy has been to focus on the core businesses or market segments of diabetes care, women's healthcare (mainly, hormone replacement therapy [HRP]), human growth hormones, and industrial enzymes. The company introduces new products simultaneously in three markets; Japan, Europe and the United States.

ENVIRONMENTAL POSTURE OF THE COMPANY

The company has a long history of environmental awareness and management starting in 1974 when the Environmental Affairs Department was established. In 1995, the company issued its first environmental policy. In 1976, for the first time ever, sludge from fermentations was reused as agricultural fertilizer. Ten years later, the Danish Act on Environment and Genetic Engineering required government approval of genetically modified microorganisms and the processes involved. In 1987, Novo Nordisk began production with genetically modified microorganisms. In the next year, public environmental awareness increased, and the company faced a new set of environmental challenges and demands from environmental and consumer organizations, customers, consumers, and the media. In 1989, an internal task force called the "Green Group" was established to respond to the new environmental demands and to coordinate activities. Two years later, the company organized the first of a series of annual visits by representatives of leading environmental organizations to company sites. In 1991, the company signed the ICC Business Charter for Sustainable Development. In 1993, the corporate environmental affairs department was reorganized and the Corporate Environmental Board was established.

The environmental policy of Novo Nordisk is centered on a belief that everyone must care for the environment and natural resources. It is committed to constantly improving its environmental performance as part of its ambition to be a good corporate citizen. The company has signed the International Chamber of Commerce's "Business Charter for Sustainable Development." Its commitment to the environmental policy is demonstrated through the pursuit of the following goals:

- To minimize the impact of the company's operations on the environment by developing more environmentally sound processes and minimizing emissions, consumption of raw materials and energy

- To strive to set high standards of environmental performance

- To educate and motivate the employees to comply with the policy

- To seek the cooperation of all suppliers and contractors to ensure that the goods and services they provide are environmentally sound

- To communicate openly, both internally and externally, the company's annual environmental performance

DRIVERS OF ENVIRONMENTAL MANAGEMENT

For Novo Nordisk, four important drivers led to an emphasis on environmental issues: governmental regulation, increasing public awareness of environmental issues, demands from environmental and consumer organizations, and demands from customers, consumers, and the media.

ENVIRONMENTAL PRACTICES

Environmental performance management, environmental information management, incorporation of environmental issues in the new product development process, and environmental organization structure are the four environmental practices that are noteworthy with respect to Novo Nordisk. The company uses its own environmental performance index called the "Eco-Productivity Index," which measures the ratio of sales turnover to input consumption. The higher the indexes, the higher the rate at which inputs are converted into sales. From 1990 to 1993, the company increased its Eco-Productivity Index for energy by 33 percent, for water by 31 percent, and for raw materials by 19 percent. For packaging materials, the indexed performance increased by 19 percent for the bio-industrial group and by 35 percent for the healthcare group. These increasing trends in eco-productivity are due to heavy investments in research and development, which lead to increased use of genetically modified microorganisms capable of utilizing inputs more efficiently.

For monitoring environmental performance, data are collected on the outputs to the environment, such as discharges of nitrogen, phosphorus, and organic material. The company handles liquid wastes through a dual strategy of recycling a higher proportion of fermentation sludges as agricultural fertilizer, and by making major investments in effluent treatment. Overall, recycling of liquid waste increased from 25 percent in 1990 to 43 percent in 1993.

As part of a comprehensive environmental communications program, the company organizes a series of annual two-day visits by environmental stakeholders. To achieve the objectives relating to safety, health and the environment, the company identified a total of 22 targets for the following activities:

- use of life-cycle assessments
- environmental management
- environmental compliance
- consumption of raw materials, water and energy
- discharge of nutrients in liquid waste
- packaging materials
- distribution
- injuries and occupational diseases
- animal experimentation
- laboratory activities
- technology transfer and biodiversity
- environmental communications and training
- the scope of future environmental reporting.

ENVIRONMENTAL ORGANIZATION

In 1993, the Corporate Environmental Board (CEB) was established which was responsible for corporate environmental policy and strategy. The CEB reports to the Corporate Executive Group, which is chaired by the CEO. The healthcare and bio-industry business groups, Corporate Environmental Affairs (CEA), and a number of specialist groups spread throughout the organization advise the CEB. The overall environmental management is coordinated by CEA, which is a corporate staff function consisting of four main units: Environmental Services; Environmental Affairs Department; Occupational Heath and Safety; and Risk Management. Environmental performance is a line management responsibility. Line managers are responsible for day-to-day operations, and for compliance with the company's environmental policy and with government regulations and permits. The ongoing challenge for revamping the environmental organization structure is the integration of existing systems into certified environmental management system.

LESSONS LEARNED

The following key lessons can be discerned from this case study:

- An experiential approach to environmental management as demonstrated by a considerably long history of environmental awareness is important.

- An unique environmental performance system as indicated by the development of a customized composite index called eco-productivity can assist efforts

- A proactive approach to environmental management as can be seen from the setting of specific targets for future environmental performance for outcomes, inputs and processes is critical for success.

- An "open" approach of communicating environmental information to the general public is desirable.

The case also suggests that an open corporate culture has an important influence on the propensity of the company to incorporate environmental issues into the firm's strategic decision-making exercise. The reliance on objective measures for monitoring, controlling, and reengineering environmental operations is also critical to recognize. It is important to consider the current organizational climate, as shaped by the influence of stakeholders such as customers, government, and consumer organizations, while deciding on environmental issues.

OSCORNA

COMPANY BACKGROUND

Oscorna of Ulm, Germany is a manufacturer of all-natural fertilizers used primarily by the home gardener. Oscorna was founded in 1935 by Mr. H. Steiner, who used discarded pig bones as the key ingredient in fertilizer. In 1952, Oscorna's manufacturing and corporate offices were moved to Ulm, Germany, where they reside today. Mr. Steiner was an environmental activist — something quite unusual in the 1930s. Mr. Steiner's vision of environmental protection is still the driving force for Oscorna operations today.

ENVIRONMENTAL PHILOSOPHY

Oscorna has repeatedly experienced that environmental activism, as a corporate philosophy is not always cost effective when viewed from a short-interval perspective. For example, in past years German law had allowed the chromium content of garden fertilizer to range between 0.05 and 0.11 percent. Oscorna in contrast has never allowed more than a trace amount of chromium in their fertilizer. This stringent specification cost Oscorna a great deal of lost profit to maintain, but it was in line with their corporate philosophy. Recently, the law was changed to allow < 0.02 percent chromium content in fertilizer products. Of course, Oscorna was able to meet these more stringent requirements at no additional cost. Frequently, a longer-term perspective must be adopted when considering environmental cost management and analysis.

How can a small company like Oscorna be environmentally proactive and remain competitive? The two keys to success for Oscorna seem to be effective advertising and market segmentation. From a pure cost perspective, Oscorna could never compete against a giant conglomerate like Hoechst AG, even if environmental issues played no role in their product planning. But the environmental issue gives Oscorna a distinct advantage over their competitors, both large and small, that cannot easily be duplicated.

Oscorna's market situation is one in which 80 percent of their customer base are consumers willing to pay a higher price for a superior product. Please note that the all-natural, environmentally sound ingredients used by Oscorna make the product of perceived high quality and especially sought after by the home gardener.

As the environmental laws in Europe have been tightened, Oscorna's production costs have been dropping relative to their competition. Production costs have been decreasing relative to the competition because the all-natural ingredients create less unwanted chemical byproducts. The resulting cleanup and disposal costs for residuals have been exceedingly low.

SUPPLIER SELECTION

The search for all-natural, environmentally friendly ingredients has turned global in order to find the best and yet most cost-efficient alternatives. Even with the global sourcing of ingredients, the cost of these purchased materials is often higher than Oscorna would like. This cost problem heightens the importance of consumer education. Customer sensitivity must be cultivated carefully.

Oscorna has found that the desired sense of social and environmental responsibility must flow through the entire fabric of the company. From a pure business perspective, the use of specifications that far exceed legal requirement and put the company at a cost disadvantage to their competitors does not always make sense. Oscorna must constantly communicate through word and deed the environmental and social vision of the company throughout the organization structure. It cannot just be

Oscorna's products that are socially responsible. For example, Oscorna also has an implemented policy of guaranteed employment with their workforce. Such social policies also play well with their customer base and reflect the social reputation that Oscorna has carefully cultivated.

Oscorna participates in the environmental certification audit development of Europe (EMAS) and intends to apply these criteria to its suppliers worldwide. This supplier audit will examine all aspects of supplier environmental effectiveness, such as, safety, production processes, waste disposal, and many other areas.

The role played by effective communications is a critical one for Oscorna. Communication of social goals to consumers is a market tool that allows Oscorna to charge a premium price for a high quality product. Oscorna applies for nearly all available awards or certifications that attest to their product quality, environmental responsibility, or both.

But communication plays a critical internal role as well. Effective communication of corporate philosophies and goals not only educates all internal functions concerning the importance of these goals to Oscorna's success but also aligns the strategies of the internal functions with each other and corporate philosophies. Cost containment and environmental responsibility can, in the short term, be viewed by a function as mutually exclusive goals; in the short term these goals frequently are divergent. But over the past 60 years Oscorna has experienced time and again the wisdom of their environmental corporate philosophy.

LESSONS LEARNED

- A longer-term perspective must be adopted when considering environmental cost management and analysis.

- The search for all-natural, environmentally friendly ingredients has turned global in order to find the best and yet most cost-efficient alternatives.

SIDLER GMBH AND CO.

COMPANY BACKGROUND

When the automotive industry speaks of interior lighting for automobiles, they often mean Sidler, the market leader in interior lighting, ashtrays, and other interior trim (see Figure 24 for Sidler product sales). Why has Sidler been so successful? Sidler knows how much their customers depend on quality, Sidler is ISO 9001 certified, delivery and total value — on zero-defect manufacturing, and sound, economical logistics even

within their small market segments (see Figure 25 for a listing of Sidler's customers). Few suppliers have perfected their expertise in luxury interior lighting, roof control units, and ashtray modules like Sidler. Application of two-color injection molding serves as just one example of Sidler's manufacturing talents (see Figure 26 for a limited picture of Sidler's import volumes from within the European Union).

Automobile consumers are changing their outlook; comfort and safety are becoming the fashion, and no wonder. People are spending more of their time in an automobile. Luxury lighting, fresh air, and an expanded range of functions are gaining importance among the driving public. As a result, these same issues are being addressed by leading worldwide vehicle manufacturers.

The principal objective in automobile lights and air systems is to have all systems functioning smoothly without having to memorize a bulky owner's manual. Sidler has been trying to address these issues. Their interior lighting and ashtrays meet the highest standards of quality, ergonomics, and design. Sidler integrates complex electronic systems and storage compartments into dashboards and consoles that please the eye and are simple to use.

Figure 27 presents the revenue ratios for each of Sidler's three main product groups. Contained within the "lighting" product line are inside lights, comfort lights, hazard flashers, brake lights, and navigational lights. Contained within the "inside equipment" product line are ashtrays, change boxes, restraint holders, and cup holders. Contained within the "other products" lines are security systems, motor coverings, ventilation components, and sound-deadening components.

ENVIRONMENTAL SUPPLIER MANAGEMENT

Sidler has found that there is no correlation between an environmentally sensitive supplier and a good supplier. Sidler feels that good suppliers can and should be environmentally sensitive and effective. Toward this end, Sidler has several processes in place to encourage their good suppliers to become environmentally effective. Figure 28 presents the environmental process for the supplier requirements during first demand of new material. Please note both the cross-functional responsibility and cooperation required for the process to function effectively.

Figure 29 provides a schematic of the supplier requirements during conclusion of an agreement with external service personnel. Once again, this process is viewed as cross-functional in nature with several functions assuming implementation responsibility for various relevant segments of the process.

FIGURE 24

SIDLER PRODUCT SALES

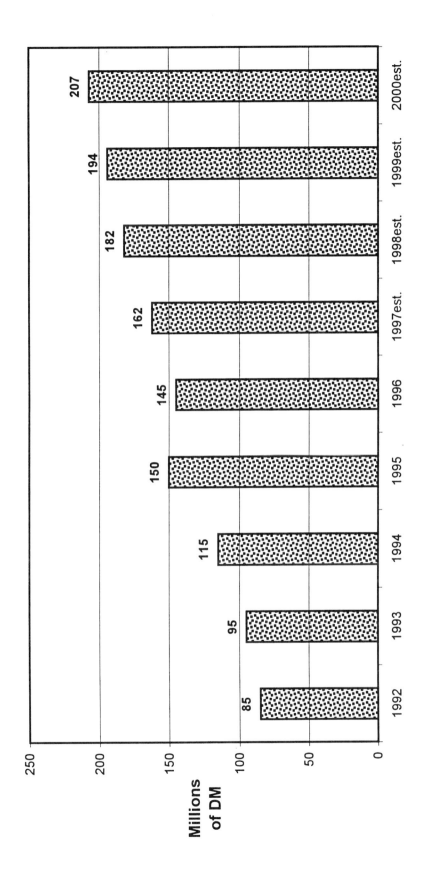

FIGURE 25
SIDLER CUSTOMERS

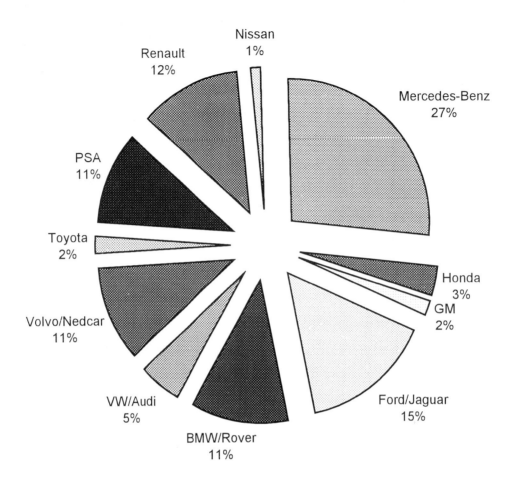

Figure 30 portrays the environmental aspects as they impact the conclusion of an agreement with suppliers. Note that explicit preference is given to suppliers who clearly demonstrate their environmental efficiency and planning. After many years, Sidler has come to the conclusion that environmental concern is much akin to cost consciousness, and environmentally aware suppliers should be both effective and low cost. As an example, notice the weight given to life-cycle cost assessment as the most effective way to truly examine the cost saving accrued through environmental initiatives.

Sidler has tried to assist their suppliers' environmental efforts by involving them as early as possible in the product development stage, maintaining longer-term cooperative relationships with key suppliers, and developing material and other specifications that exhibit enough flexibility to incorporate supplier ingenuity. Sidler views the over-specification of materials as stifling to supplier input on environmental issues.

LESSONS LEARNED

- The cross-functional relevance of environmental supply chain management is ensured by its direct impact on the supplier selection and management processes.

FIGURE 26
SIDLER IMPORT VOLUMES

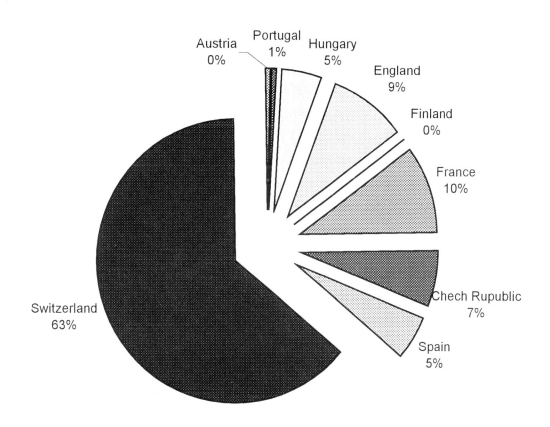

FIGURE 27
SIDLER REVENUE RATIOS

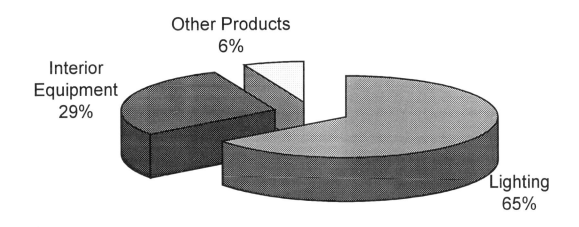

FIGURE 28
SUPPLIER REQUIREMENTS: FIRST DEMAND OF NEW MATERIAL
C = Cooperation
I = Implementation Responsibility

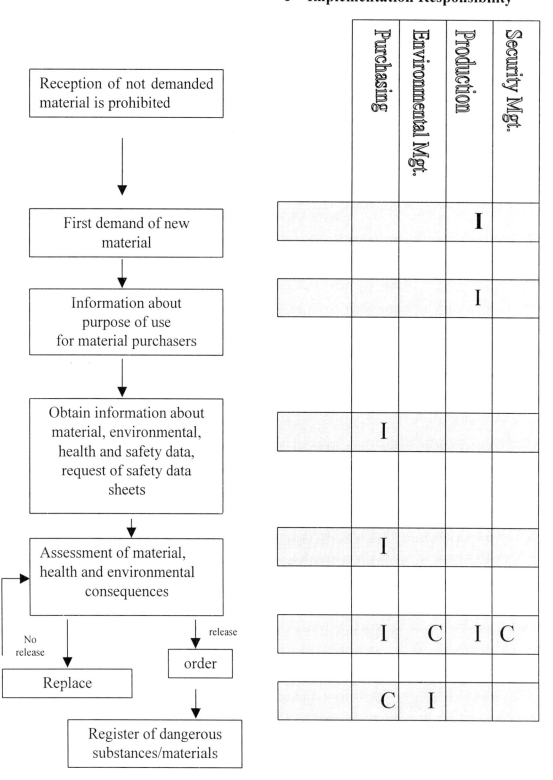

FIGURE 29
SUPPLIER REQUIREMENTS: CONCLUDING AN AGREEMENT WITH EXTERNAL SERVICE PERSONNEL

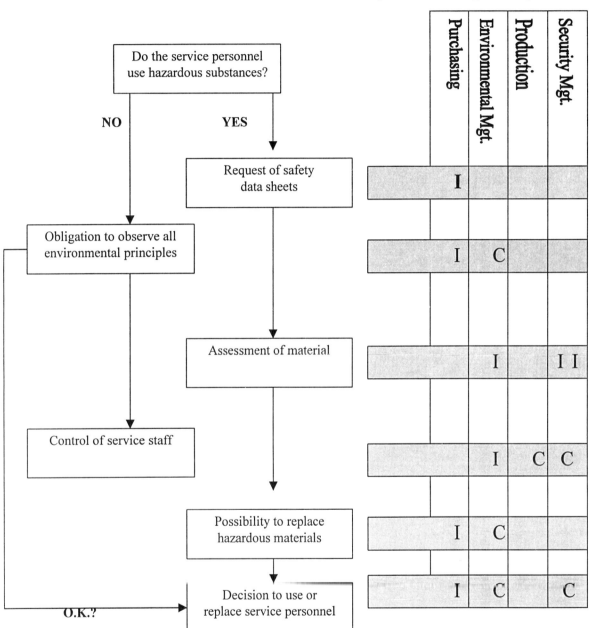

C = Cooperation
I = Implementation Responsibility

FIGURE 30
SUPPLIER REQUIREMENTS: CONCLUSION OF AN AGREEMENT WITH SUPPLIERS

C = Cooperation
I = Implementation Responsibility

	Purchasing	Environmental Mgt.
Criteria for supplier selection: ❖ Suppliers who support environmental cooperation and facilitate exchange of environmental data will be preferred. ❖ Companies, which are EMAS or ISO 14000 certified, will be favored above others. ❖ Life-cycle assessments: long-lived and recyclable products, cooperation, design for recyclability ❖ Control of chemicals ❖ Optimized handling of waste ❖ Free-of-charge returns system for packing materials	I	C
Assessment of all data	C	I
Decision about future orders	I	

UZIN GEORG UTZ GMBH & CO.

COMPANY BACKGROUND

Georg Utz founded UZIN in 1911. In the 1950s, Willi Utz established the excellent reputation of UZIN adhesives, and since the 1970s, UZIN cement compounds and tiling materials have assumed an outstanding position on the German and European markets.

Today, UZIN's other strengths are in their close relationship with the wholesale trade, and in the way they promote the efficiency of their target group — specialist flooring and tiling craftsmen.

The basic principles behind UZIN's corporate philosophy include preparing the way for an economically successful future for the trade and craftsmen, which in turn also ensures their own existence and future growth. Concerning environmental issues, the product has always been the first focus of efforts with the process falling in line to satisfy product needs.

Since March 1994, UZIN has joined those companies that have been certified to ISO 9001. This procedure is perceived as endorsing the quality of all UZIN company divisions and as an essential prerequisite for good product and service quality. ISO 14000 certification is viewed as inevitable and desirable; UZIN is working toward being certified in 1998. UZIN has been proactive in trying to meet or exceed all regulations before the formal regulations appear. This "early start" provides them with the time to meet all regulations in a cost-effective and market-efficient manner.

UZIN's commitment to environmental efficiency runs through all departments and functions; from product development and production via application technology and specialized counseling to marketing. They provide top quality service in the interests of their customers. The customer market has always been the focus of UZIN's environmental efforts. These efforts have in some cases meant higher prices, but these new prices have always been justified to the customer in cost savings, for example, less adhesive per square meter of tile or carpet used.

ENABLERS OF ENVIRONMENTAL SUCCESS

Research and development is the basis for the creation of top-quality products for the success of specialist craftsmen. Expert chemists, laboratory assistants, and engineers research and develop custom products that comply with the changing requirements of the trade, such as, time-saving installation and environmental compatibility. In fact, safety for the craftsman customer is a major selling point of environmental product issues. Also, recycling issues are becoming increasingly important. Even though they are not yet required to do so,

UZIN wants to develop adhesives that can be recycled easily. For example, adhesives must be capable of being recycled with the rug after extraction from the floor.

Every item is securely and efficiently packaged. The procedures are fully automated for filling the tiling adhesives grout leveling compounds into their containers, and for packaging these onto pallets ready for transport. A computerized central warehouse is responsible for fast, economical delivery to all their customers in Europe. Internally, a great deal of effort has been placed on reducing the amount of packaging needed in both incoming and outgoing product.

The proper adhesive is carefully matched to each situation. Special adhesives are developed and recommended for special floor coverings. This is how the customer finds his tailor-made UZIN product. Fully developed formulas guarantee the outstanding technical properties for each particular application. For a long time UZIN has been considerate of the environment in all their development work, and they offer solvent-free products for every situation. As mentioned before, recycling the products will be a major issue in the year 2002. All waste from demolished housing cannot be thrown away. UZIN knows that they will be held responsible for a disposal plan for the adhesive left on old rugs.

Product environmental quality begins with the raw materials, which are selected according to stringent criteria and are subject to constant environmental controls. They are processed precisely according to each particular formula to create top quality brand products. The manufacturing process is monitored throughout all phases. Highly sensitive measuring instruments not only ensure that products comply with precise environmental guidelines for each production stage, but also produce complete documentation.

Investment in advanced production technology is viewed as critical to environmental effectiveness. UZIN invests in advanced machinery in order to guarantee a constantly high environmental quality standard for all products, together with reliable delivery and environmentally friendly production. UZIN's major processes are physical and not chemical. As such, a critical concern is the environmentally friendly cleaning of those processes.

The newly completed powder blending works is equipped with state-of-the-art production technology. The two independent production lines meet the increasing requirements for quality and quantity without sacrificing environmental efficiency, while the central control point is the heart of the whole plant. This is where experienced staff work to control and monitor internal production logistics and precise compliance with the complex formulae.

Many UZIN activities are centered on providing a service for the wholesale trade and craftsman. UZIN's market-oriented range of products and comprehensive services programs are specifically designed to meet the needs of the specialized trade sector:

- Application advice, by phone or on-site, uses expert knowledge to ensure that individual practical requirements are effectively and efficiently satisfied

- The UZIN expert advisors are the direct contact partners for the entire customer base

- Training courses extend knowledge about new product systems and latest developments

- Business management seminars focusing on marketing, sales promotion, and company management provide their customers with an opportunity for further training

- Information and advertising literature help the wholesale trade and the craftsmen to present their expert image to their own customers.

What does UZIN see as major environmental policy trends? Recycling was the issue in 1997. As a result, waste that needs to be destroyed by burning has been reduced dramatically. The future trend seems to be the development of product that can be safely burned by electrical generation facilities without emission of toxic or other waste by-products.

LESSONS LEARNED

- Environmental goals first should be product driven, then process driven. Changes to products and processes that enhance environmental effectiveness and efficiency should be directly linked to customer needs and satisfaction.

- The corporate organizational structure should be set up so that environmental efficiency runs through all departments and functions.

WHIRLPOOL CORPORATION

COMPANY BACKGROUND

Whirlpool Corporation is the world's leading manufacturer and marketer of major home appliances. It employs over 40,000 workers and is headquartered in Benton Harbor, Michigan. In 1994, the company earned total revenues of $8.1 billion and net profits of $330 million. Its future strategy is to shape and lead the emerging global home appliance industry. It has global procurement centers that buy materials and components to support its worldwide production facilities. Its strategy is to centralize most of the sourcing and local components and spare parts to the nearest production centers. In 1996, Whirlpool introduced a horizontal-axis washer that consumes 50 percent less water than currently existing vertical-axis washers. Also in that year, the company launched a world-class small capacity no-frost refrigerator that contains no CFCs and is designed to meet the needs of the national markets of Asia and Latin America.

DRIVERS

Several drivers may explain the environmental posture of the company. Concern of the customers about the "environmental friendliness" of Whirlpool products is one such example. The move towards CFC-elimination due to official deadlines imposed by the 1987 Montreal protocol is another example. The company's global presence has exposed it to regulations in several countries. For example, in Europe environmental laws require manufacturers to provide for the disposal of packaging free of charge to the consumer. This has prompted the company to develop a reusable multi-package system for built-in ovens.

ENVIRONMENTAL MANAGEMENT

Several examples illustrate the company's consideration of environmental issues in business decisions. For example, its five main plants that manufacture finished appliances have reduced the amount of water used to make appliances by 72 percent since 1976. As a participant of the Green Lights Program, Whirlpool is committed to retrofitting 90 percent of its U.S. office, manufacturing, and warehousing space with energy-efficient lighting and technology. Between 1987 and 1994, non-hazardous waste decreased 33 percent while production increased 23 percent. Whirlpool uses returnable packaging for parts and materials in some of its plants and has made agreements with packaging suppliers to encourage the return of packaging materials. It also participates in environmental awareness programs such as Earth Day. Environmental spending in 1994 was in the areas of risk reduction (6.9 percent), waste management (10.9 percent), and compliance (82.2 percent). Its Corporate

Environmental Council formulates, updates, and continuously improves their policies and the mechanisms and processes that enable compliance. The senior manager in charge of each business unit, product team, or company facility has ultimate responsibility for effecting compliance within his or her domain of influence.

ENVIRONMENTAL PRACTICES

Whirlpool is studying ways to increase the potential of recyclability for its products through such measures as product design and material specification. An environmental product-assessment tool called "Eco-Design" evaluates the environmental impact of an existing or new product in a variety of categories, including raw materials required to build the product, water and energy consumption during manufacturing and use, recyclability of parts, and ease of dismantling.

Audit teams consisting of environmental engineers and technicians conduct audits of facilities every three years to measure plant performance against applicable laws, regulations, industry standards, and self-imposed environmental goals. Also, measures of environmental performance of plants are assessed through internal audits and amount of fines paid.

In Europe, the recycling of appliances is outsourced to a German company, Rethmann. Customers return their appliances to dealers who send them to Rethmann for recycling. In the United States, the recycling of appliances is outsourced to Appliance Recycling Centers of America (ARCA) who recycle, recondition, resell, and also replace older refrigerators with more energy-efficient models in "early retirement" programs.

LESSONS LEARNED

The company boasts of many examples of pioneering environmental efforts:

- Whirlpool was the first company in the United States to develop a procedure for recovering CFCs released during servicing of the refrigerators

- Technological innovation by Whirlpool's European engineers — a portable CFC-recovery unit

- Whirlpool won the competition sponsored by U.S. public and private utility companies to produce the Super Efficient Refrigerator Program (SERP) in February 1994. It began production of this refrigerator and followed it by a second-generation of its kind in July 1995.

- Unique recycling efforts "at home" — the manufacturing plant actually maintains its own recycling facility in-house with a sorting operation that processes all trash generated from plant operations.

CHAPTER 4: GENERIC TOOLS FOR ENVIRONMENTAL SUPPLY CHAIN MANAGEMENT •

LIFE-CYCLE ANALYSIS

The LCM Process Flow Chart used at 3M was presented in Figure 2. This chart focuses on characterization and management of risk as well as business opportunities for its products. For example, developing products such as inhalers without CFC is viewed as a business opportunity. The LCM Team is composed of a technology leader, marketing leader, process engineer, manufacturing engineer, toxicologist, environmental engineer, and a liaison person from procurement for product responsibility. Pre-screening questions pertaining to potential market size, options for products (aerosol versus pump, etc.) and user characteristics are identified. Logical connections among these elements are made through flow charts. A risk matrix composed of generic questions on risk management and an opportunity matrix is then constructed.

LCM Opportunity Matrix

The LCM Opportunity Matrix consists of two sub-matrices: the business opportunity matrix (see Figure 9) and market advantage matrix. The business opportunity assessment examines the environmental (energy and resources), health and safety aspects of the product in four stages: customer use, final disposal, materials acquisition, and manufacture. For example, if the product in question is a CFC-free solvent, first an examination from the customer use perspective is undertaken. Representative issues include whether the product is a non-ozone depleting chemical, has low or no global warming potential, and does not contain VOCs (volatile organic compounds). The product is evaluated from the energy and resource perspective as well as from a health and safety point of view; for example, is the final product flammable. Next, an evaluation of environmental, health, and safety aspects during disposal are assessed. Ultimately, something must be done at the time of disposal with recycling of the end product being the most preferred option. At the materials acquisition stage, composition of the ingredients frequently has special implications for emissions. To attain the objective of reducing emissions, a supply chain focus is maintained by extending the environmental inquiry backward to purchasing and suppliers. The optimal ingredient from a "sustainability" perspective is the preferred choice. For example, if there is a choice between a solvent-based tape versus

"Hot Melt," hard metal that is melted and extruded as a type of tape, representative considerations in the final choice include verifying the presence of thermal oxidizers and effluents, health and safety risks associated with the product because of composition of the material, and safety issues in packaging, handling, and transporting. For example, the presence of cadmium and heavy metals can pose health concerns and logistics problems. This interest in environmental, health, and safety aspects during the different stages of the product life-cycle is extended to include first- and second-tier suppliers. For example, suppliers are asked questions regarding energy consumption and resource utilization. At this stage, a great deal is asked of manufacturing. In each manufacturing area, typical questions posed are:

- Is there an environmental impact?
- If so, does it constitute risk?
- What can be done to manage the risk?
- Can the risk be turned into a business advantage?

Risk Opportunity Matrix

The risk opportunity matrix is used throughout the life cycle of a product, prioritizing and refocusing risk management activities (see Figure 10). For example, there is a business opportunity for using a CFC substitute such as HFA (Hydro-Fluro Alkanes) for cleaning electronic boards. The risks associated with the use of HFAs include its constituting ingredient of hydrogen fluoride, which is a concern, and the in-process handling of HFAs. HFAs also have advantages associated with their characteristics of a low contribution to global warming, and non-VOC. This aspect, when cross-referenced to the risk opportunity matrix, can serve as a marketing tool.

ENVIRONMENTAL RISK ANALYSIS

Environmental risk analysis is a systematic, predictive tool for identifying and evaluating hazards associated with business processes. It is most commonly used for the evaluation of manufacturing processes. Companies that are further along in the formal adoption of environmental risk analysis are beginning to emerge. For example, Novartis is a company in the advanced stage of using environmental risk analysis to evaluate the risks and benefits associated with products and processes. The following description of the procedures involved in environmental risk analysis is based on materials provided by Novartis.

The example covered is that of a chemical manufacturing process in the company. Safety guidelines, regulations, and technical instructions facilitate the control of commonly occurring safety problems. However, chemical manufacturing processes frequently involve unique combinations of chemicals, plant and process conditions. Therefore, a systematic procedure, such as environmental risk analysis, is required for ensuring and maintaining process safety. "Hazard" is defined as a physical situation with a potential for harm such as injury, damage to property, damage to the environment, or any combination. Risk is a hazard that has been evaluated with regard to the probability of occurrence of an incident and the severity of the possible consequences. In the chemical industry, common critical areas of hazards are chemicals, reactions, plants, energy, personnel, and external influences.

The environmental risk analysis of a process involves a progression along distinct stages of development including research, chemical development, pilot plant, project realization, start-up, and permanent operation. The objectives of risk analysis are to improve the level of safety in processes, to include new experiences, in-house or external of the process, and to re-evaluate residual risks. Examples of key activities in each development stage of environmental risk analysis are shown in Figure 31. In the research stage, an initial process is selected and subject to the verification of risks associated with the chemicals in use and their reactions. While considering the new product, basic data are collected, and decisions relating to the technical process, path of chemical synthesis, reaction procedure, and the choice of process is made by taking into account the potential safety implications. If there is a possibility of new hazards, the existing risk analyses are revised. New hazards can occur due to a variety of reasons such as modification of the process, change of equipment, change in materials that are used, or repairs to the process.

A pilot plant, usually a laboratory-scale prototype, is used to decide on equipment requirements, process control, and capacity requirements relating to scale-up operations.

A team of at least two employees carries out the actual risk analysis. The team is usually composed of experienced professionals with interdisciplinary skills. For the purpose of risk analysis, the team seeks cooperation from process donors (those handing over the process), future users, responsible project engineers, technical experts, and a moderator, if required, who is not a team member but who has the knowledge of risk analysis methodology.

In Figure 31, the different steps in environmental risk analysis for each process are presented. Obviously, deviations from safe working conditions cause hazards; consequently, a systematic search for hazards can only take place once safe working conditions are ensured, process limits defined, and consequences of deviations from limits are understood. The chemicals involved in the process, intended reactions, and criteria for safe processing are important factors to consider in risk analysis. Compilation of data provides the basic information on the inherent hazards of the chemicals and the processes. This forms the basis for the entire risk analysis. The data are gathered during the process development stage using available knowledge from practice and the literature. The systematic search for hazards, risk evaluation, planning for safety measures, and evaluation of residual risk are all based on safe process conditions and the established limit values for the processes.

The systematic search for hazards is the most creative step in environmental risk analysis. Each process should be considered based on operating and plant practice. Plant specific data and drawings should be available for analysis. It is important to ensure that the drawings correspond to actual situations. A site inspection is conducted with special attention being paid to critical details and hazards, such as cables carried over sharp edges, leaks, scale formation, dismantled fittings, and influence from neighboring plants. Many of these details may not be found in drawings. In the systematic search for hazards, the critical areas of chemicals, reactions, plants, energy, personnel, and external influences are investigated for deviations from safe process conditions. These deviations are listed together with statements of cause and effect. Checklists can be effective for this purpose especially in the specialty chemicals industry; they incorporate experiences accumulated over decades. Additional methods for specific hazard investigations can then be applied depending on the critical area in which the key risks lie.

The procedures are concerned mainly with chemical production and synthesis plants. In contrast to these, in infra-structural facilities, chemical hazards are not so much in the forefront but the properties of the substances used and their undesired reactions must be known. Here, risk analysis ensures the safe operation of the physical processes, such as the generation or conversion of desired forms of energy. For this reason, risk analysis concentrates on the examination of technical failures.

Although it is true that each of these infrastructural facilities is an individual case, they can be classified into certain categories (such as storage, packing/dispatch stations, heating/cooling facilities, effluent/off-gas treatment, waste disposal). For most of these categories, the comprehensive operation of the plant or facility is the focus, but this does not take away the responsibility to consider additional safety measures that may be necessary.

FIGURE 31

KEY ACTIVITIES IN EACH DEVELOPMENT
STAGE OF ENVIRONMENTAL RISK ANALYSIS

Development Stage	Examples of Key Activities
Research	Establishing a process or working method, which is adequate in view of the unknown risks of chemicals and reactions to be used
Chemical Development	Acquisition of basic data Inclusion of safety criteria when choosing synthesis path, technical process, reaction procedure and work-up methods
Pilot Plant	Scale-up Equipment requirements Process control
Plant Introduction/Production transfer Investment Proposal/Project Realization	Selection of site Plant layout Analysis of interactions Control concept Measurement and control Safety elements
Start-up	Start-up and shut-down instructions Testing of safety elements
Permanent Operation	Health protection Maintenance concept Training concept Maintenance of safety levels Emergency response

In the risk evaluation step, the statements on cause and effect of the hazards are taken and risks are evaluated with respect to severity and probability of occurrence. The main reason for evaluation with respect to severity and probability of occurrence is to indicate the possible consequences. In Figures 32 and 33, examples are given of severity categories and typical rating of probability.

The assessment of severity provides a basis for later decisions on appropriate safety measures. In practice, evaluation of probability is more difficult because non-quantifiable influences are of significance such as maintenance, leadership, training, and motivation. Since the assessment of probability is judgmental and contains subjective biases, care is taken to include information from past experience, comparison to similar situations, statistical evidence, and quantitative evaluation using decision analysis techniques.

Proposed safety measures should reduce the recognized risk to an acceptable level. The main goal of planning for safety measures is to reduce severity. With chemical processes, this is often achieved by means of process development. Thus, there is a need for conducting risk analysis in the early stages of process and product development. Technical safety measures also can reduce severity. For example, the use of fire alarms and sprinklers in warehouses, installation of second barriers, and explosion suppression or relief can reduce severity. Measures of instrumentation and control can only reduce probability of incident, but not its severity. Therefore, safety measures should be planned with the following objectives in mind:

- select processes with lowest risks
- reduce risks by using technical measures
- install alarm systems

FIGURE 32
EXAMPLES OF SEVERITY CATEGORIES

Category	People	Effect on Environment	Material Value
Low	Slight injury	Short-term noise pollution	Minor machine damage, loss of a batch
Medium	Injury without permanent disability	Water discoloration, smell	Plant damage without prolonged plant shutdown
High	Injury with permanent disability	Dead fish, defoliation, poisoning of waste water treatment plant	Loss of a plant or building

FIGURE 33
TYPICAL RATINGS OF PROBABILITY

Probability	Technical Failure	Human Error	External Influence
High	Failure of online analytical probes	Mix-up of products; identical packaging; Wrong interpretation of verbal instructions	Frost, rain
Medium	Failure of measuring elements	Mix-up of products; identical packaging; Wrong interpretation of written instructions	Prolonged power failure; transport accident
Low	Failure of redundant methods and/or fail-safe elements	Mix-up of products; delivered by fixed pipe-work; wrong interpretation of written instructions, double-checked	Aircraft crash on chemical plant

- take organizational and personnel safety measures
- prepare emergency measures.

The matrix of measure for a dangerous reaction (Figure 34) displays the possibilities for safety measures according to their application and mode of action.

In the last step of the environmental risk analysis, it is necessary to take into account the risk that remains in spite of safety measures. Generally, there are no valid criteria for assessing residual risk. Technical considerations, economic, business, environmental, and sociopolitical viewpoints are taken into consideration for this purpose. The "Safety Principles" implemented by the executive committee should expressly require that safety must not be compromised for productivity and economy. The evaluation of residual risks can lead to a need for further safety measures, and in extreme cases, even to cancellation of proposed processes.

Apart from safety measures that cover only risks from known hazards, other types of risks include risks that are consciously accepted, risks that are identified but misjudged, and risks that remain undetected. If the risk is judged to be too uncertain or too high, the risk analysis must be repeated from the appropriate step — search for hazards, planning for measures, or even compilation of data. A review of risk analysis is a valuable auditing instrument prior to the introduction of a new process to a plant. If process modifications are envisioned, the review must start with the corresponding basic data.

A process is acceptable from a technical safety point of view if a comprehensive environmental risk analysis is carried out, available knowledge and scientific methods are used, and safety measures are taken that are in conformance with the law, current state of technical development, and the company safety regulations and guidelines.

ORGANIZING FOR ESCM

Firms have implemented several types of organization structures for their environmental supply chain management efforts. The following description of the organization structure of Novartis' environmental protection department is abstracted from a case study published by Wise (1995).

In the wake of developments such as de-layering the number of management levels, teamwork, and efforts to encourage individual initiative and risk taking, it is all the more important that economic, social, and environmental performance goals be clearly defined and responsibility for meeting these goals be unequivocally assigned. To meet the goal of accountability, Novartis implemented the organization structure as shown in Figure 35.

As can be seen from this figure, the President and Board of Directors are assigned to oversee all activities to ensure that the company follows the path of economically, socially, and environmentally responsible entrepreneurship. The CEO and Executive Committee, as the highest executive body, bear the overall responsibility, not only for economic, but also for social and environmental performance. To achieve these objectives, corporate policies and governing principles are formulated, responsibilities are clearly defined, ethical and intellectually qualified managers are appointed, and regular supervision and control is exercised.

FIGURE 34
MATRIX OF MEASURES FOR A DANGEROUS REACTION

	MODE	OF ACTION	
Field of Application	**Eliminative measures**	**Preventive measures**	**Emergency measures**
Technical	Different path of synthesis	Process control alarm systems	Explosion relief venting, sprinklers
Organizational		Process control by operators	Emergency services
Personnel	No employees in danger zone	Education, training, instructions for handling process deviations	Instructions for emergency

FIGURE 35
NOVARTIS OLD ORGANIZATION CHART

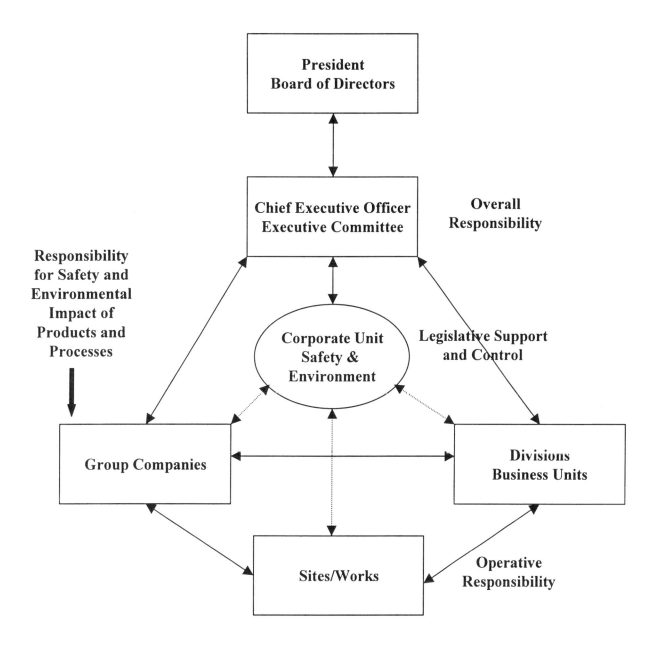

The heads of divisions and their deputies are responsible for the safety and environmental compatibility of products and manufacturing processes, as well as for procuring and disseminating relevant information. The heads of the group companies, as representatives of the executive committee in their respective countries, have overall responsibility for the compliance of their group's activities with local safety and environmental legislation, company policies, directives, and guidelines in these fields.

The site/works managers are responsible for all operational matters at their site, including the safety, health, and environmental performance with the right to stop production or any other business activity if there are concerns about safety, health or environmental protection. The Corporate Unit Safety and Environment is a staff function reporting to the CEO and Executive Committee. It oversees and strives to continually improve safety and environmental performance through:

- procurement and documentation of safety and environmental data
- elaboration of safety and environmental standards
- promulgation of scientific knowledge and engineering know-how
- support and assistance from safety and environmental specialists
- assessment of safety, environmental compatibility, and regulatory compliance

In the Novartis group of companies, adequate controls and follow-up are provided for proper implementation of environmental policies. Certain control functions are inherent in the responsibilities assigned to the heads of divisions, business units, group companies, and plant sites. Experienced staff and technical experts, as well as safety and environmental specialists, support these managers. The heads of larger group companies have their own technical department with safety, health, and environmental specialists who maintain close contact and share experiences with their parent — company counterparts. The divisions and business units ensure that relevant information, which is technically and factually correct, is disseminated and that a comparable standard of safety, health, and environmental protection is achieved worldwide.

The Corporate Unit Safety and Environment, a staff function of the Executive Committee, undertakes independent safety and environmental audits of all larger manufacturing sites. Through these corporate audits, Novartis strives to achieve performance that exceeds assessing the environmental management systems, as is intended in the European Union's Eco-Audit Directive. Not only does the company audit against internal standards, which often go beyond regulatory requirements, but their experts also make an assessment of the technical standard and of future needs of the facility. This includes a comparison with best available practices and techniques, some of which have been developed within the company by its own safety and environmental specialists. Any deficiencies and shortcomings are corrected expeditiously, and the auditor's advice and recommendations must be followed and implemented within reasonable time.

To summarize, Novartis' culture is largely determined by the "Vision 2000" and by common values which have been adopted by all employees. These values are expressed by governing principles for safety and environmental protection, which in turn are embodied in rules of conduct for various situations. The responsibilities for setting safety and environmental goals and objectives, and for attaining them, have been clearly defined. In uncertain cases, specialists can be relied upon for expert advice and guidance. Unsolved problems are researched using scientific methods. Experience and newly acquired know-how are codified and documented in an easily comprehensible form, so that they can be readily applied to situations and translated into action. The adherence to the rules of conduct and the acceptance and implementation of new findings are periodically checked, and the necessary corrections are initiated in the case of deviations.

In response to the strategic goals of waste minimization, an evaluation of the re-mediation process was undertaken; this led to the adoption of a new project management orientation using teams in the Environmental Protection Department. Four regional re-mediation teams were created with new procedures and facilities, all reporting to the same organization. A new management philosophy instilled a sense of ownership to all members of the team.

Teams were developed utilizing three distinct operational sections: the External Affairs Section, which took responsibility for dealing with "outside" stakeholders such as EPA and local communities; the Technical Section, which provided scientific investigation, design, and construction support; the Regional Affairs that provided administrative support, communicated with upper management, and provided backup for the other two sections. The new organization structure is shown in Figure 36.

Section managers reported to a director-level, on-site sponsor. The sponsor's role is to coach the team and assume an advisory role. This resulted in flattening of organization layers. Section associates with disciplinary expertise were assigned to assist section managers who trained and encouraged the team to deal with external customers and support agencies. Management levels were de-emphasized and team building was encouraged. The teams obtained general direction and guidance from a management team of sponsors and the director of environmental protection.

FIGURE 36
NOVARTIS NEW ORGANIZATION CHART

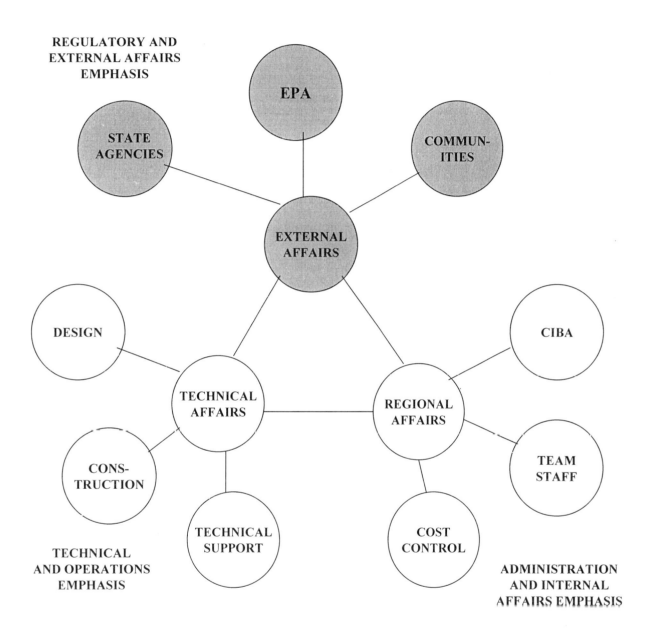

REGULATORY AND
EXTERNAL AFFAIRS
EMPHASIS

EPA

STATE
AGENCIES

COMMUN-
ITIES

EXTERNAL
AFFAIRS

DESIGN

CIBA

TECHNICAL
AFFAIRS

REGIONAL
AFFAIRS

CONS-
TRUCTION

TEAM
STAFF

TECHNICAL
SUPPORT

COST
CONTROL

TECHNICAL
AND OPERATIONS
EMPHASIS

ADMINISTRATION
AND INTERNAL
AFFAIRS EMPHASIS

In the first year of operation, the department improved project cash flow by $17 million and cut departmental expenses by $1.5 million. In 18 months of operation, the teams resolved difficult technological and legal issues and controlled project costs and schedules. They managed their own personnel, information systems, and facility issues with little or no supervision.

The advantages of the empowered team over the traditional "project manager" approach were as follows:

- Creative, synergistic problem solving produced better re-mediation alternatives.
- A customer approach to agencies and the public improved relationships.
- Resident experts depend less on consultants or critical decisions.
- Managers had a backup and the workload was spread more evenly.
- Empowered teams seem to have higher morale.

ENVIRONMENTAL ECO-AUDIT

The environmental audit of 3M is carried out in the wake of several broad trends such as a high level of inspections and enforcement, increased public participation in environmental activities, expanded definition of hazardous waste, regulation of non-hazardous waste, and increasing pressure for waste minimization. The goals of the environmental program are as follows:

- assess and document compliance status
- help improve overall environmental performance of facility
- assist facility management
- increase environmental awareness

- improve environmental management system
- protect from potential liabilities
- optimize environmental resources
- ensure systems are in place for continued compliance

The emphasis on environmental audit programs has resulted in benefits such as better compliance with regulations, protection from environmental liability, improved management of liability issues, reduction in regulatory fines, and support and endorsement from EPA. As shown in Figure 37, the environmental audit process follows three stages: pre-audit activities, on-site activities, and post-audit activities.

The facility audit process typically starts with pre-audit preparation by the audit team members. The goal is to understand all the issues before the site visit. Each audit is tailored to the specific needs of a facility. Auditors team up with facility personnel to help ensure a thorough audit. Preplanning includes the following activities:

- Notifying the operating unit management

- Contacting the facility management and scheduling the audit

- Selecting the audit team. Usually, the team comprises three members: a full-time auditor who is also the team leader charged with the responsibility of coordination and control of the audit process, an appropriate environment engineering services (EES) person, and a specialist who has expertise in an identified area of concern.

FIGURE 37
ENVIRONMENTAL AUDIT PROCESS

Pre-Audit Activities	On-Site Activities	Post-Audit Activities
Approval	Orientation meeting	Finalize audit report
Scheduling	Conduct audit (1-5 days)	Track audit findings
Team selection	Write draft audit report	Conduct survey to assess audit program
Prepare facility for audit	Develop audit follow-up action plan	General counsel review and audit follow-up
Review records, regulations	Conduct audit exit meeting	Final audit closure

88

- Reviewing the federal, state and local regulations

- Reviewing the facility environmental management plan with the EES person in order to update knowledge of facility issues and their status

- Reviewing the environmental engineering and pollution control (EE & PC) facility files and corporate computer databases to become familiar with the issues at the facility. The facility files are part of the total compliance program designed to maintain and control critical records. It is a centralized filing system containing up-to-date records on permits, process and facility monitoring, emergency plans, and other regulatory activities.

- Understanding the requirements of current federal, state and local regulations. The *Federal Register* and other sources are used for federal regulations coverage. Due to the number of states in which 3M operates facilities, a variety of sources are used to identify state-specific regulations.

- Involving the company's internal auditing on selected audits

- Consulting as appropriate with the company's senior environmental counsel

The on-site audit process starts with an initial orientation meeting. At this meeting, the purpose and scope of the environmental audit program is reviewed. A plan of attack for proceeding with the audit is specified. The team then reviews the objectives of 3M's environmental audit program, discusses potential agency concerns, and reviews past environmental audit findings and compliance history from the time of the last audit. The team discusses planning of the audit follow-up and post-audit survey, and schedules the data and time for the wrap-up meeting.

The actual audit can last from one to five days, depending on the size and complexity of the facility. The following activities comprise the audit process:

- *Facility walk-through:* The audit team inspects all indoor and outdoor locations of the facility

- *Facility paper audit:* During the site visit, the team reviews pertinent documents and operating procedures with facility personnel to verify that all systems are in place and functioning as intended

- *Environmental Management Systems Review:* Throughout the audit, facility personnel are questioned to determine the effectiveness of the environmental management system. A high-level system is essential if continuous compliance is to be assured

- *Inspection checklists:* Checklists are used as a guide to help the auditors identify areas of concern. Areas covered by checklists include air, water and wastewater, solid and hazardous waste.

Before leaving the site, the auditors generate a draft audit report detailing the findings and recommendations for improvement. The report is the basis for the "next exit" meeting discussion and issue resolution planning. The senior environmental counsel reviews the draft report. At the conclusion of the audit, the draft report is reviewed at the site by facility and environmental department personnel. Related to each finding, a remedial action plan is drawn, persons responsible for solution are identified, and a due date for completion is assigned. The audit group also develops facility self-inspection checklists that site personnel can use to continually monitor their operations.

The post-audit follow-up activities include: drafting the final audit report, tracking audit findings, issuing a post-audit facility survey, review of findings by senior environmental counsel, and an audit wrap-up. From the information gained from the exit meeting, the final audit report is compiled. The Office of General Counsel, under whose direction the audit is conducted, reviews this report. The actual audit report is a confidential and attorney-client privileged document and is targeted to be issued within two weeks of completion of the audit. The report is addressed to the facility manager who coordinates the follow-up and keeps the audit team leader informed of progress.

The company also uses an audit computerized tracking (ACT) system to generate pre-audit letters, audit letters, and reports. This facilitates on-time closures on issues that are still open by generating a form letter requiring action. For example, every month the ACT system issues confidential status reports on all open audit findings. The reports are sent to the environmental department contact person, facility manager, and senior environmental counsel until all audit findings are resolved. If audit findings are not resolved within a reasonable period, then higher levels of management and senior environmental counsel are involved for resolving the pending issues. The added benefit of the tracking system is the preservation of an audit and documentation trail.

The environmental department vice-president issues a survey to the facility manager two months after an audit has been conducted. The responses from the survey help in identifying any problem areas and judging the effectiveness of the audit program. Senior environmental counsel reviews all the audit findings who also provide legal advice and direction throughout the follow-up process. Finally, as part of audit wrap-up, a confirmation letter is sent to the operating unit management indicating that all audit findings have been satisfactorily resolved.

ENVIRONMENTAL POLICY DEPLOYMENT FRAMEWORK

In Figure 38, a strategy deployment framework, which includes environmental aspects, is presented. Developing corporate strategies involves setting corporate — level goals and identifying firm-specific sources of competitive advantage. An example of a corporate goal is environmental sustainable development. Attainment of this goal involves consideration of product aspects, process aspects, regulatory aspects and financial aspects. Within each category, there are objectives and specific action programs to attain them; for example, environmental issues play an important role in conceptual design in the product category. The conceptual design may involve setting targets that require the coordination of marketing and an integrated product development team (IPDT). Environment-related targets may pertain to simplicity in design, environmentally friendly packaging, and ease of disassembly. To attain these objectives, action programs such as design for the environment (DFE), recycling, reuse and life-cycle management may be utilized. In the process category, there are objectives relating to the manufacturing process, materials, machines and workers. Issues relating to environmental impact, safety and health are pertinent in this category.

In the regulatory aspect category, issues relating to storage and disposal of hazardous materials and compliance with environmental laws are important. Using tools such as LCM, costs from a "total life-cycle" point of view are considered. Tools such as total cost of ownership can be used for this purpose.

In Figure 39, a planning framework pertaining to attaining the objective of sustainable manufacturing is presented in detail from a "decisions" or process point of view. Using a framework similar to the "House of Quality," a matrix of enablers versus strategic objectives is developed. The rows of the matrix correspond to the sustainable development goals, and the columns represent the different desired objectives. To the extreme right of the matrix is the performance of the firm relative to the competitors on individual elements of sustainable development goals. For example, in Figure 39, the "cross marks" in the row pertaining to design for disassembly, the sustainable development goal relating to design and development, means that the firm needs to improve its performance in this category relative to the competition. The cells corresponding to the row and column are marked as "high," "medium," and "low" impact to designate the influence of a specific enabler in attaining a specific goal. At the top (roof) of the matrix is the correlation between

the attainment of different objectives, with positive correlation representing possible attainment of two objectives simultaneously, and positive correlation representing the tradeoff in attaining the two objectives. The tools needed to facilitate the enabling process are also noted to the left of Figure 39. Between the functions within the firm, supply chain integration can be facilitated through the use of tools such as value engineering, technology development, and make-buy decision making. The supply base can also be included with the firm's supply chain integration effort. For this purpose, tools such as environmental auditing and life-cycle analysis can be used. There is an influence of the environmental decisions throughout the supply chain, from design and development to logistics and customer support. The pressures on the supply chain also drive similar prerequisites for the supply base. In other words, a strategic orientation of the buyer firm can influence a relationship between the buyer and its supply base.

In summary, the process of incorporating sustainable development goals in corporate strategy has been summarized in two stages in Figures 38 and 39. In Figure 38, the connection between overall strategy and macro elements of sustainable development goals (product, process, regulatory and financial) is presented. This linkage is further expanded into micro-decision elements in Figure 39 to present the implications of incorporating environmental issues on functional and integration-related decisions.

FIGURE 38
STRATEGY DEPLOYMENT FRAMEWORK

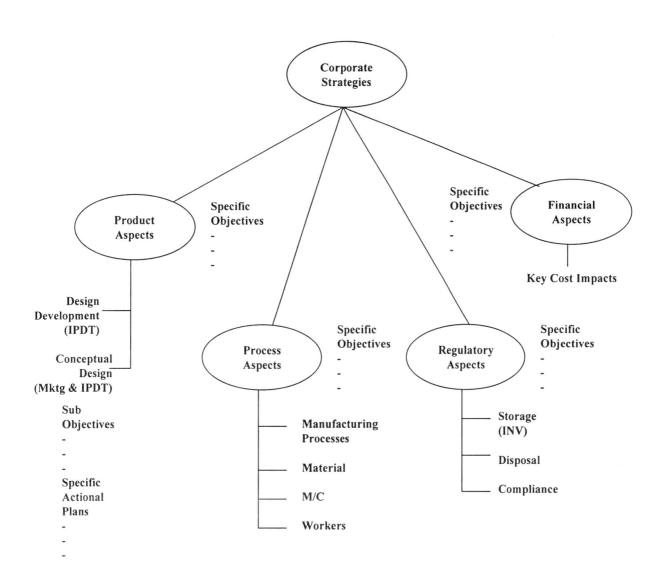

FIGURE 39
SUSTAINABLE MANUFACTURING: A PLANNING FRAMEWORK

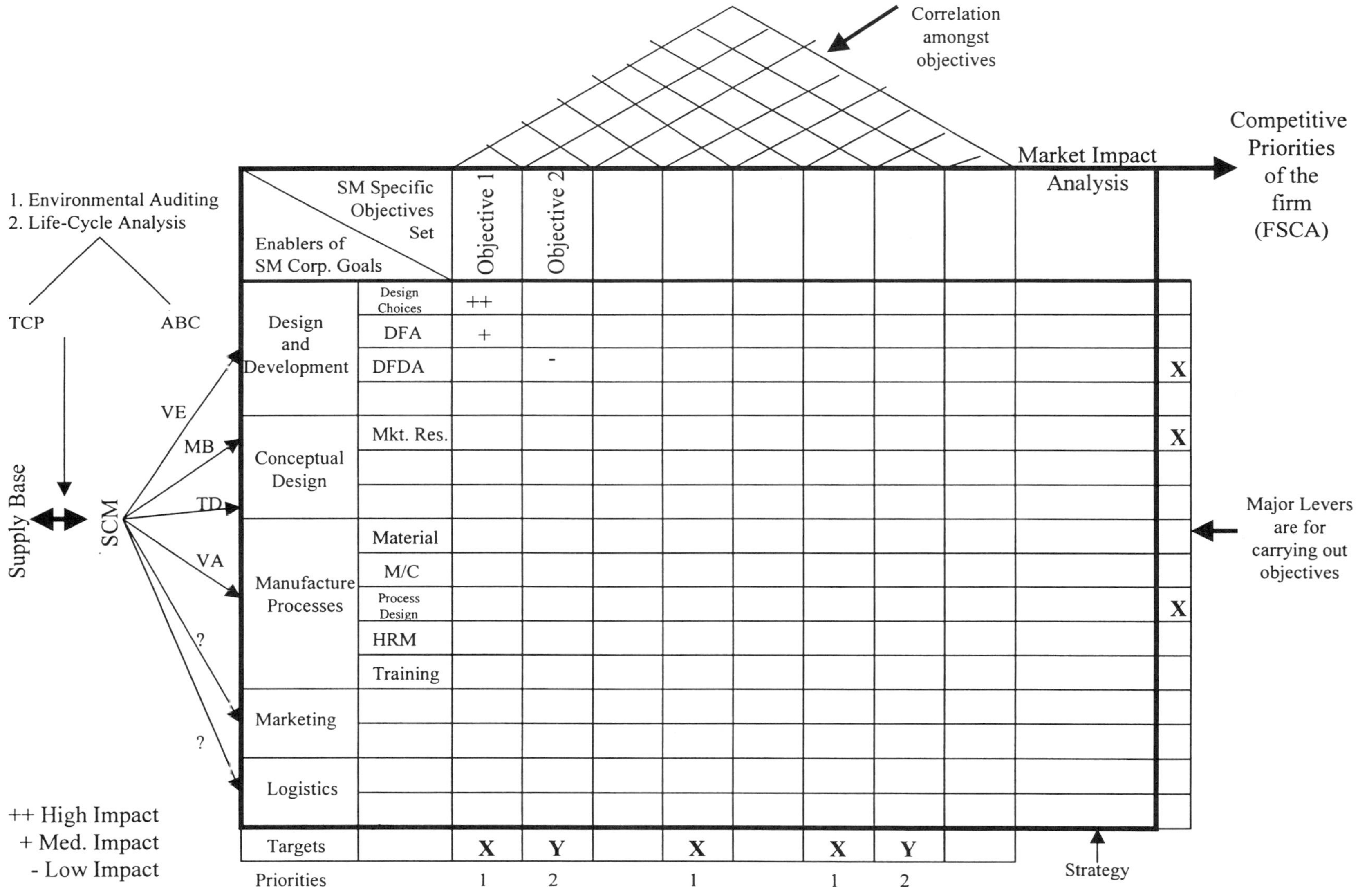

Competitive Priorities of the firm (FSCA)

Market Impact Analysis

Major Levers are for carrying out objectives

Correlation amongst objectives

SM Specific Objectives Set

Enablers of SM Corp. Goals

		Objective 1	Objective 2						
Design and Development	Design Choices	++							X
	DFA	+							
	DFDA		-						X
Conceptual Design	Mkt. Res.								
Manufacture Processes	Material								
	M/C								X
	Process Design								
	HRM								
Marketing	Training								
Logistics									
Targets		X	Y	X	X	X	Y		
Priorities		1	2	1	1	1	2		

Strategy

1. Environmental Auditing
2. Life-Cycle Analysis

TCP — ABC — VE — MB — TD — VA — SCM

SCM

Supply Base

++ High Impact
+ Med. Impact
- Low Impact

92

CHAPTER 5: CROSS-CASE ANALYSIS •

CROSS-CASE ANALYSIS

The case studies described in Chapter 3 yielded 16 themes relating to environmental supply chain management (ESCM) as shown in Figure 40. As can be seen from Figure 40, life-cycle management appears to be the most important environmental practice emphasized by the firms covered in this study. It is interesting to note that firms from a wide cross-section of industries find this tool to be useful in the planning of products and processes.

Environmental performance measurement is another popular theme in the cases covered in this study. Several companies had customized environmental performance measurement systems that were adapted from uniform standards such as ISO 14000 and other European standards. Figure 40 also highlights some of the less popular tools. For example, uniform global environmental strategies appear to be less popular among the firms covered in this study. This is perhaps due to differences in maturity and awareness of environmental issues in the different regions of the world, and the lack of prior experience in developing and implementing global environmental strategies.

Across the two regions of North America and Europe, the pattern of emphasis on environmental issues is different. As can be seen Figure 41, European firms have made sufficient advances in environmental man agement by going beyond environmental compliance and garnering a reputation for being environmentally-friendly. On the other hand, firms in North America are only beginning to realize the benefits of actively considering environmentally based competitive strategies.

Although there has been a distinct lag effect in the adoption of environmental strategies between European firms and North American firms, the drivers faced by these firms are the same. These drivers include the intensity of global competition, the global reach of markets, trends relating to product and process standardization, the transfer of "best practices," increasing levels of consumer awareness, and cross-cultural diffusion.

MAJOR PROPOSITIONS

While, the current trends affecting environmentally conscious manufacturing are issues relating to re-manufacturing, reuse, process waste, human resource programs (such as empowerment, waste re-mediation teams,

and employee suggestion programs), and inbound logistics, the future holds new trends that will change the face of environmentally conscious manufacturing. These trends are described below as propositions:

Proposition 1: The level of consumer awareness of environmental issues will increase rapidly.

The influence of this trend has already been felt; consider the example of products relating to healthcare. Because of stringent product labeling standards and media exposure, there is considerable awareness among consumers of environmental topics that were heretofore too technical.

Proposition 2: Firms will place an increasing emphasis on environmentalism in the evaluation of effectiveness of business processes.

Currently, there are several companies that use sophisticated environmental performance measurement schemes. This trend is expected to increase because an orientation toward business processes is common among most firms. Therefore, one can assume that environmental issues should be considered at each business process level.

Proposition 3: The transfer of knowledge among subsidiaries of large firms will increase rapidly.

Firms will place an increasing emphasis of environmentalism in the evaluation of effectiveness of business processes through:

• Knowledge diffusion
• Uniform environmental standards

Proposition 4: Four major inter-organizational forces drive environmental supply chain activities. Those forces are governments, suppliers, customers, and competitors (Carter and Ellram, 1998).

While the literature review suggests a set of internal and external drivers of environmental supply chain activities, this case research has provided further multi-variate empirical examination in order to identify which of these

FIGURE 40
ENVIRONMENTAL SUPPLY CHAIN MANAGEMENT (ESCM) THEMES

	ESCM THEMES	3M	Ciba-Geigy	Daimler-Benz	Eli Lilly	Grundfos	Novo Nordisk	Whirlpool
					CASES			
1.	Recyclability					X		X
2.	Reuse/Re-manufacturing					X		
3.	Waste Elimination/Disposal							
4.	Proactive Environmental Orientation			X				
5.	Environmental Information Management			X		X		
6.	Global Environmental Strategy					X		
7.	Life-Cycle Management	X	X	X	X	X	X	X
8.	Environmental Performance Measurement		X		X	X	X	X
9.	Green Packaging					X		
10.	Process Technology							
11.	Materials/Systems Sourcing							
12.	Supplier's Environmental Capability	X		X	X	X		
13.	Design for the Environment			X				
14.	Environmental Risk Assessment		X		X	X		
15.	Compliance with Environmental Regulations (Reports, Standards etc.)	X						
16.	Environmental Eco-Audit	X	X			X		X

94

	ESCM THEMES	UZIN	Honda	Oscorna	Sidler	Denso	DEKRA	Hoechst
					CASES			
1.	Recyclability	X	X			X		
2.	Reuse/Re-manufacturing	X	X			X		
3.	Waste Elimination/Disposal		X			X		X
4.	Proactive Environmental Orientation	X	X	X	X	X	X	X
5.	Environmental Information Management		X	X		X	X	X
6.	Global Environmental Strategy		X	X		X		X
7.	Life Cycle Management		X	X	X	X	X	
8.	Environmental Performance Measurement	X	X	X	X	X	X	X
9.	Green Packaging	X	X	X		X		
10.	Process Technology	X	X	X	X	X		X
11.	Materials/Systems Sourcing	X		X	X	X		X
12.	Supplier's Environmental Capability				X	X		X
13.	Design for the Environment	X	X	X		X		
14.	Environmental Risk Assessment		X	X	X	X	X	X
15.	Compliance with Environmental Regulations (Reports, Standards etc.)	X	X	X	X	X	X	X
16.	Environmental Eco-Audit	X	X	X	X	X	X	X

FIGURE 41
DRIVERS FOR ENVIRONMENTALLY CONSCIOUS MANUFACTURING[1]

REGION	Cost	Quality	CORPORATE Environmental Compliance	STRATEGY Environmental Reputation	Innovation (Product/ Process)	Differentiation
Europe$_{Current}$	+	+	+	+	+	+
Europe$_{Future}$			+++	+++	++	++
North America$_{Current}$	++	++			++	+
North America$_{Future}$	++	++	++	++	++	+

[1] + signifies the intensity of the relationship

factors are the key driver(s) of environmental purchasing activities. Identification of the primary inter-organizational drivers of environmental purchasing can help managers allocate limited resources toward management of those parts of the supply chain that are having the greatest impact on a firm's environmental activities.

The case study research also suggests that upstream members of a supply chain can limit the effectiveness of environmental supply chain management activities due to the uncertainty of the availability of resources, poor quality of environmentally efficient inputs, and insufficient coordination with suppliers of these inputs.

Proposition 5: Upstream members of a supply chain can affect environmental supply chain activities, and purchasing managers must take action to manage these effects.

The case studies suggested that government regulations drive many of the environmental purchasing activities. However, it proved logical that a firm's customers, suppliers, and competitors — its supply chain — are also affecting environmental purchasing activities.

Proposition 6: The higher the quality of environmentally friendly inputs, the greater will be the level of environmental purchasing (Carter and Ellram, 1998).

Increased vertical coordination through the supply chain should affect environmental purchasing activity, where vertical coordination exists along a continuum from one-time, spot market transactions through equity integration. The case study data suggest that as vertical coordination increases, so too will the rate of adoption of new technology. While not all environmental purchasing activities fall under the formal rubric of technology, it is reasonable to consider the manner in which new environmental purchasing programs are adopted and implemented in a similar fashion. For example, the introduction of new environmentally efficient resources into the conversion process might require purchasing managers to act as a liaison between process engineers and the suppliers of these resources.

Proposition 7: The greater the supply uncertainty, the greater the level of vertical coordination between buyers and suppliers (Carter and Ellram, 1998).

The case study data suggest several propositions based upon the concept of environmental uncertainty. One set of propositions suggests that as environmental uncertainty increases, vertical coordination will increase. This proposition indicates that vertical coordination will in turn be positively correlated with the degree of supply uncertainty. Herein, supply uncertainty is defined as the uncertain availability of environmentally efficient inputs.

In addition to supply uncertainty, the case study data indicated that the criticality of the environmental resource affected the level of vertical coordination between buyers and suppliers. For example, a firm tended to expend greater efforts with suppliers of critical process inputs, as opposed to suppliers of a generic, readily available item.

CHAPTER 6: MANAGERIAL IMPLICATIONS •

In a recent study, Sarkis (1995) noted several practices that were indicative of superior environmental performance, such as:

- Pursuing a business goal of attaining a corporate reputation for environmental excellence

- Practicing pollution prevention at the source

- Forming alliances with major stakeholders such as environmental groups, regulators, academia, suppliers and customers

- Developing environmental goals that are future-oriented — for example, anticipating current environmental trends that may turn into future environmental standards

- Avoiding suppliers that take ecological or environmental shortcuts or both — for example, suppliers that provide materials that are not biodegradable recyclable, reusable, etc.

- Empowering employees to assume responsibility for environmental protection

- Encouraging employees to take preventive and corrective actions that enhance superior environmental performance of the company

- Installing performance measurement systems that capture the environmental impact of the company's products, processes and technologies

Even beyond the broad array of environmental practices is an underlying coherent environmental strategy that a firm pursues. This environmental strategy should not be developed in isolation, but should be linked to corporate-level competitive priorities. In previous chapters, a generic framework for deploying environmental strategy based on corporate strategy was introduced and explained. Broadly, firms compete on the basis of the competitive priorities of cost, quality, product and process innovation, and other forms of differentiation such as customization, responsiveness, and timeliness. Recently, two other forms of differentiation have begun to appear; environmental efficiency (for example, compliance) and environmental reputation. Firms with healthy environmental records are likely to enjoy more customer goodwill as compared to firms with poor environmental records. On the other end of the scale, some

firms (Diamler Benz, for example) compete on the basis of being able to tap the latest environmental technologies for their new products. The relationship between corporate level competitive priorities and environmental issues is shown in Figure 42.

In Figure 42, the corporate generic strategies are shown in the columns. The rows correspond to various environmental issues in product and process design. Environmental issues which impact the effectiveness of one or more corporate strategies are marked with an "X." Environmental issues for which there is a direct impact on the achievement of one or more corporate goals are shown separately (X1 or X2). For example, the environmental issue of reuse and re-manufacturing has a direct impact (X1) on achieving the goals of product/process innovation, customization, responsiveness and timeliness in product design, and environmental reputation. Reuse and re-manufacturing also have an indirect effect (X2) on achieving cost and quality goals. Similar interpretations can be made for other environmental issues.

While Figure 42 establishes the link between corporate goals and environmental strategies, similar linkages can be made between environmental strategies and environmental SCM. For example, relating to the common types of environmental strategies pursued by firms (such as, recycling, reuse, re-manufacturing and waste elimination, minimization and/or disposal) are several supply chain management decisions such as material acquisition, manufacturing, distribution, packaging, and customer support. For instance, in material acquisition, a conscious effort to increase the percentage of procured items that are recyclable is indicative of a recycling strategy. Similarly, a sourcing strategy that emphasizes the purchase of items with high reusability content is typical of a reuse strategy. Purchasing has a key role in locating sources of items and arranging for transportation of those items in a manner suitable for re-processing in a re-manufacturing strategy. Waste elimination and disposal strategies that may affect the purchasing function include scrapping of waste, sorting of nontoxic waste for subsequent incineration, and use of biodegradable packaging.

Purchasing has an increasingly important role in its contribution to a firm's environmental strategy. A recent survey of purchasing executives (Min and Galle, 1997) found that:

FIGURE 42
RELATIONSHIP BETWEEN CORPORATE STRATEGY AND ENVIRONMENTAL ISSUES

Environmental Issues in Product/Process Design	Cost	Quality	CORPORATE STRATEGY			
			Environmental Compliance	Environmental Reputation	Innovation (Product/ Process)	Differentiation (Customization, Responsiveness, Timeliness)
Reuse/Re-manufacturing	X_2			X_1	X_1	X_1(Product design)
Recyclability	X_2		X_1	X_1	X_2	X_2
Process Technology	X_1		X_1	X_1, X_2	X_1	
Materials/Systems	X_1			X_1		
Supplier Capability	X_1		X_1	X_1		

X_1: indicates direct impact; X_2: indicates indirect impact

- liability for disposal of hazardous materials, cost for disposing hazardous materials, and regulations were the top three environmental factors that were important for a buying firm's choice of suppliers

- more than half the respondents indicated that their company had an environmental auditing program; however, only 31.9 percent of the respondents include suppliers' environmental capability as part of their suppliers quality assurance criteria

- conforming to regulations on hazardous items, packaging materials costs and package disposal costs were the three top factors that affected a buyer's environmental packaging strategy

- high cost of environmental programs, uneconomical recycling, and uneconomic reusing were reported as the three top barriers to environmental purchasing

These findings indicate that environmental purchasing strategies appear to be in their infancy stage in the United States. Even among the early adopters, the majority seems to pursue environmental goals to avoid violations of environmental statutes. The use of proactive environmental programs as an aid to supplier selection, supplier development and supplier quality assurance is distinctly lacking in widespread adoption. Purchasing also has a major responsibility in implementation of a recycling strategy. It must specify guidelines for identifying those items that should be recycled and assign responsibility for the collection, sorting and disposal (sale, reuse or remanufacture) of recycled items. To facilitate effective recycling programs, purchasing must conduct training programs and educate its employees on recycling issues.

Despite global efforts to reduce waste relating to packaging materials, too few purchasing professionals require innovative packaging materials, such as low density and biodegradable packaging, as part of the company's environmental purchasing strategy. In the future, stricter laws may mandate the use of environmentally friendly packaging in virtually all materials. Companies such as Hewlett Packard and Xerox, which are known for purchasing excellence, have already made inroads in innovative packaging of their inbound and outbound materials. A similar trend was also found in the case of Grundfos and Honda in this research.

There have been other attempts to propose generic environmental supply chain management strategies and link them to manufacturing strategy. Research has proposed a model that links the four ESCM strategies of life-cycle management, waste reduction, re-manufacturing and recycling/reuse to three categories of manufacturing strategy — product, process and technology. Figure 43 summarizes the implications of ESCM for product, process, and technology choice.

The implications of the linkages in Figure 43 are that different environmental supply chain management strategies have different impacts on the components of manufacturing strategy. The LCM approach has a proactive environmental outlook on products, processes and technology. This approach has two critical components: gathering of accurate environmental-impact related data, and the integration of such information in the future purchase of products, processes and selection of appropriate technologies.

The waste reduction strategy has important purchasing-related implications such as product standardization and simplification, and the use of materials that reduce scrap and defect rates. Manufacturing processes that reduce waste, monitor waste generation, and reduce overall inventory levels are preferred. Technology acquisition choice must consider options that facilitate substitutability decisions for materials.

Supplier development strategies must consider simplified product structures and bills of materials that facilitate remanufacture of components and end items. Manufacturing processes that are easily disassembled are preferred. Acquiring technology for disassembly, separation and reliability testing are salient technological features of supplier development strategies.

Recycling strategies must consider the purchase of modular product structures with interchangeable parts. Firms must develop an infrastructure for recycling. Acquiring technology for recycling, separation and disassembly are salient technological features of recycling strategies.

Just as there are implications of environmental strategies on corporate strategies and sourcing strategies, there are similar implications on the strategic activity of joint buyer-supplier new product and process development. The environmental implications on each stage of the new product development (NPD) process — concept development, process design, fulfillment and after sales marketing are shown in Figure 44.

As can be seen in Figure 44, the environmental impact of suppliers in the NPD process is early and substantial. For example, in the concept generation stage, at least three important environmental issues must be considered: the development of simplified product structures for purchased items, substitutability of purchased materials and components, and purchased products' potential environmental impact. To facilitate consideration of these issues, tools such as life-cycle management, design for the environment, and supplier environmental development can be used. The implications for purchasing are substantial at each and every stage in the NPD process. That is, all stages have a potential impact on purchasing.

Finally, the environmental implications of common decisions on operational considerations and strategic considerations such as supply base management and supply chain management are shown in Figure 45. Three common purchasing practices will undergo widespread change in the future to include environmental issues: identification of capable suppliers, domestic versus global sourcing, and the acquisition of systems.

CONCLUSIONS

This report summarized the key sourcing drivers for considering environmental issues, described several methods and tools, including company-specific methods, employed in several leading-edge firms, presented generic methodologies for important environmental

tools, and offered implications for purchasing and supply chain management. The accumulated evidence suggests that environmental and, in particular, environmental supply chain management issues will gain tremendous importance in the future. In Europe, trends toward environmental supply chain management are already in place. Although an average U.S.-based firm may not be thinking along environmental issues while developing sourcing strategies, pressures from the global marketplace, including proactive firms based in the United States, are likely to influence other firms to adopt a more active environmental strategy.

The results of this research were mixed in terms of impact of environmental supply chain management issues on strategic purchasing decisions. While some leading edge companies are successful in including environmental capability as a distinct criterion for evaluating suppliers, other firms do not seem to be assigning the same degree of importance to environmental issues. Similarly, in leading-edge firms new product development activities involve key suppliers at the earliest development stage. In fact, key suppliers are expected to contribute and eventually spearhead the design for environment initiatives for products developed by the buying firms.

The deployment strategy for sustainable development, which was extracted from the case data, suggests several roles for purchasing. In the future purchasing executives must be familiar with and willing to use key environmental tools, such as life-cycle management and environmental auditing, which can impact the sourcing of materials and systems. Purchasing also needs to stay abreast of developments relating to innovative forms of environmentally sound packaging that can be used for inbound and outbound logistics. Future supplier development programs should include training modules for life-cycle cost assessment, environmental auditing of suppliers, and the use of pricing based on total cost of ownership.

A supply chain is often long and complex, consisting of several levels and dozens of members. Certainly environmental issues occur at the second- and third-tier supplier levels. Conventional wisdom states that the entire supply chain should focus itself on a similar goal — customer satisfaction. But, the complexity, length, and information inefficiencies of most chains make this focus somewhat distorted.

This report provides an empirical development of a practical model of environmental purchasing, not a theory. The model can be viewed as the first stage of identifying and formulating the leading variables that affect environmental management of the supply chain. Thus the purpose of the models presented in this chapter are to aid firms in systematically developing a managerial

FIGURE 43
IMPLICATIONS OF ENVIRONMENTAL SUPPLY CHAIN MANAGEMENT FOR PRODUCT, PROCESS AND TECHNOLOGY CHOICE

ESCM - RELATED STRATEGIES	IMPLICATIONS FOR:		
	PRODUCT DESIGN PURCHASING	PROCESS DESIGN PURCHASING	TECHNOLOGY ACQUISITION
Life-Cycle Management (LCM)	• Need to purchase for the environment • Include waste stream elements in detailed design preplanning for products • Develop and collect data from suppliers for materials standards • Develop metrics for environmental assessment of purchased items over their life cycle	• Work with suppliers to determine tangible and intangible costs and benefits for assessment data • Purchase energy-efficient equipment • Develop standards, using supplier data, for life-cycle analysis	• Acquire information technology (such as decision support systems) for accessing environmental-related data for materials and products • Develop and adjust concurrent design technology with key suppliers • Develop and use energy-efficient technology
Reduction/ Minimization	• Waste reduction is taken into account in concurrent engineering and supplier design • Purchase items that reduce scrap and defects • Simplify bill of materials for purchased products	• Purchase value-adding processes as opposed to value-detracting processes • Develop with suppliers waste monitoring systems and performance measures • Reduce inventory levels throughout the supply chain	• Acquire manufacturing technology to support value-added processes • Develop information technology and databases for making decisions on substitutability of supplier-provided materials
Re-manufacturing	• Purchase products for re-manufacturability • New product structure and bill of materials has to be developed • Encourage suppliers to design modular items with interchangeable parts • Give higher priority to supplier design options that have a higher percentage of items that are re-manufacturable	• Purchase processes that can be disassembled • Develop tools and techniques to conduct feasibility studies for the purchase of remanufactured items	• Acquire technology for disassembly and separation • Acquire technology for testing of reliability of re-manufacturable items
Recycle-Reuse	• Encourage suppliers to design products for recyclability/reusability • Supplier development issues include impact on secondary markets • Supplier packaging that is recyclable	• Develop a recycling infrastructure • Integrate purchased recycling equipment into standard manufacturing process • Build supplier network for recyclable materials (e.g., reverse logistics)	• Acquire integrated manufacturing technology with recycling stations • Acquire separation technology for recyclable and reusable materials • Encourage suppliers to substitutable material that is more recyclable and more durable

Source: Adapted from Sarkis , 1995)

FIGURE 44
INTEGRATED PRODUCT AND PROCESS DEVELOPMENT PROCESS

Tools/Methods	*Environmental Issues* / *Decisions In:*			
	Concept Development and Product Design	Process Design	Fulfillment	After/Sales Service and Purchasing
• Design for the Environment • Life-Cycle Assessment	• Simplified Product Structure Purchasing • Substitutability of Supplier Provided Materials/Components • Sourced Material's Potential Environmental Impact			
• Life-Cycle Assessment • Environmental Risk Analysis		• Choice of Process Technology • Vertical Integration through Supply Chain • Process Waste from Purchased Materials		
• Statistical Process Control • Environmental Performance Measurement			• Supplier Process Capability • Supplier Process Control • Supplier Process Performance and Feedback	
• Environmental Information Management • Strategic Alliances with Key Suppliers				• Post-sales Customer Feedback to Suppliers • Recycling • Technical Assistance • Supplier Development

101

FIGURE 45
ENVIRONMENTAL IMPLICATIONS FOR COMMON PURCHASING DECISIONS

| | *Purchasing* | *Activities:* | |
Sourcing	Operational Considerations	Supply-Base Management	Supply Chain Management

• Identification of capable suppliers (material, design)
• Global versus local suppliers (length of supply chain, environmental difference in standards, monitoring compliance)
• Acquisition of systems
	• Inventory reduction of hazardous materials used in production (strategy : JIT purchasing)
	• Implications for insurance and filing of governmental reports and forms (implication is lowering of financial risk)
		• Supplier Evaluation
		• Supplier Environmental Development
		  • Certification
		  • Qualification
		• Supplier Selection
		• Total Cost of Acquisition
		• Packaging Development
		• Supplier Environmental Benchmarking
			• Incoming material control
			• Inbound logistics
			• Containerization
			• Reverse Logistics
			• Environmental Strategy Development

paradigm for the role of supply chain management in environmental endeavors. The results must therefore be considered developmental in nature, indicating the need for extension and replication.

The case study results indicate the need for inter-functional coordination and the adoption of a value-chain perspective, including a closer relationship between purchasing and other functions. Purchasing must interface with engineering in order to ensure that materials that are specified can be recycled or reused, or to meet resource reduction goals.

While this research focused on inter-organizational factors that effect environmental supply chain management, the review of the literature indicated that intra-organizational factors have an impact, including a sincere commitment to environmental issues, successfully implemented ethical standards, the existence of managers who make a strong commitment and take personal responsibility for organizational adoption of an environmentally friendly philosophy, and the presence of adequate reward and incentive systems for employees.

Finally, an extension of this research can be used to consider the consequences of environmental supply chain management: What factors are in turn affected by environmental purchasing activities and programs? A recent investigation found a positive link between environmental performance, measured in part by pollution emissions and quality awards, and financial performance (Klassen and McLaughlin, 1996). Extrapolating this research, it seems likely that the future will prove that environmental supply chain management, including environmental purchasing, affects environmental performance.

APPENDIX A: REFERENCES •

Alexander, G.J. & Buchholz, R.A. "Corporate social responsibility and stock market performance" *Academy of Management Journal,* 1978, 21, 479-486.

Apsan, H.N. (1995). "Environmental performance evaluation: The ISO 14000 scorecard," *Total Quality Environmental Management,* 5(2), Winter, 101-106.

Arlow, P. & Gannon, M.J. "Social responsiveness, corporate structure and economic performance," *Academy of Management Review,* 1982, 7, 235-241.

Bari, D.F. (1995). "Life cycle assessment as an environmental management tool," *Ward's Auto World,* 31(11), November, 17.

Barry, J., Girard, G., & Perras, C. "Logistics shifts into reverse," *The Journal of European Business,* 1993, September/October, 34-38.

Bronstad, G.H. & Evans-Correia, K. "Green purchasing: The purchasing agent's role in corporate recycling," *1992 Conference Proceedings of the National Association of Purchasing Management,* 117-121.

Bryson, N.S., and Donohue, B.G. (1996). "EPA's proposed guidance on acquisition of environmentally preferable products and services - Will your products qualify?'" *Total Quality Environmental Management,* 5(3), Spring, 113-119.

Cairncross, F. "How Europe's companies reposition to recycle," *Harvard Business Review,* 1992, March-April, 35-45.

Campbell, S.N. and Byington, J.R. (1995). "Environmental auditing: An environmental management tool," *Internal Auditing,* 11(2), Fall, 9-18.

Carter, C. R. (1996) *Interorganizational Determinants of Environmental Purchasing: An International Comparison,* Doctoral Dissertation, Arizona State University.

Carter, C.R. and Ellram, L. (1998) "Reverse logistics: A review of the literature and framework for future investigation," *Journal of Business Logistics,* 19(1), 85-102.

Carter, J.R. and Narasimhan, R. (1996) "Purchasing and supply management: Future directions and trends,"

International Journal of Purchasing and Materials Management, Vol. 32, No. 4 (Fall): pp. 2-12.

Cavinato, J. L. (1992). "A total cost/value model for supply chain competitiveness," *Journal of Business Logistics,* 13(2), 285-301.

Craig, E. (1992). "Proactive environmental programs: Defining customers and measuring their expectations at Apple Computer," *Total Quality Environmental Management,* 2(2), Winter, 165-169.

Cysewski, J.B. and Howell, R.D. (1995). "3M international environmental management system," *Total Quality Environmental Management,* 5(2), Winter, 25-34.

Dambach, B.F and Allenby, B.R. (1995). "Implementing design for environment at AT&T," *Total Quality Environmental Management,* 4(3), Spring, 51-62.

Day, G.S. & Wensley, R. "Marketing theory with a strategic orientation," *Journal of Marketing,* 1983, 47 (Fall), 79-89.

Dean, T.J. & Brown, R.L. "Pollution regulation as a barrier to new firm entry: Initial evidence and implications for future research," *Academy of Management Journal,* 1995, 38(1), 288-303.

Dorfman, M.H., Muir, W.R. & Miller, C.G. *Environmental dividends: Cutting more chemical wastes.* New York: Inform, 1992.

Drumwright, M.E. "Socially responsible organizational buying: Environmental concern as a noneconomic buying criterion," *Journal of Marketing,* 1994, 58 (July), 1-19.

Fear, J.E. (1995). "Strengthening business with a new vision at Avery Dennison," *Total Quality Environmental Management,* 5(2), Winter, 49-55.

Fiksel, J. (1993). "Quality metrics in design for environment," *Total Quality Environmental Management,* 3(2), Winter, 181-192.

FitzGerald, C. (1994). "Environmental management information systems: New tools for measuring performance," *Total Quality Environmental Management,* 4(2), Winter, 21-33.

Gess, D. and Cohan, D. (1994). "Managing life-cycle costs: Applications and lessons learned at leading utilities," *Total Quality Environmental Management,* 4(2), Winter, 43-53.

Gloria, T., Saad, T., Breville, M., and O Connell, M. (1995). "Life-cycle assessment: A survey of current implementation," *Total Quality Environmental Management,* 4(3), Spring, 33-50.

Giuntini, R. (1996). "An introduction to reverse logistics for environmental management: A new system to support sustainability and profitability," *Total Quality Environmental Management,* 5(3), Spring, 81-87.

Gray, V. & Guthrie, J. "Ethical issues of environmentally friendly packaging," *International Journal of Physical Distribution and Logistics Management,* 1990, 20(8), 31-36.

Guiltinan, J.P. & Nwokoye, N.G. "Developing distribution channels and systems in the emerging recycling industries," *International Journal of Physical Distribution,* 1975, 6(1), 28-38.

Gupta, M.C. (1995). "Environmental management and its impact on the operations function," I*nternational Journal of Operations & Production Management,* 15(8), 34-51.

Haines, R.W. (1993). "Environmental performance indicators: Balancing compliance with business economics," *Total Quality Environmental Management,* 2(4), Summer, 367-372.

Hedstrom, G.S. and Voeller, R.W. (1993). "Evaluating your environmental audit - Moving beyond band-aids in developing corrective actions," *Total Quality Environmental Management,* 2(4), Summer, 429-439.

Huang, E.A. and Hunkeler, D.J. (1995). "Using life-cycle assessments in large corporations: A survey of current practices," *Total Quality Environmental Management,* 5(2), Winter, 35-47.

Iannuzzi, A. (1995). "Reengineering the environmental function: Making tough decisions," *Total Quality Environmental Management,* 4(3), Spring, 109-114.

Jahre, M. "Household waste collection as a reverse channel: A theoretical perspective," *International Journal of Physical Distribution and Logistics Management,* 1995, 25(2), 39-55.

Jamison, L. (1996). "Environmental purchasing-making it mainstream," *Management Services,* 40(4), April: 24-25.

Johannson, L., (1994). "How can a TQEM approach add value to your supply chain?" *Total Quality Environmental Management,* 3(4), Summer, 521-530.

Kellogg, M. "After Environmentalism: Three approaches to managing environmental regulation," *Regulation,* 1994, 1, 25-34.

Kiser, D.M. and Esler, J.G. (1995). "Kodak's safety performance indexing - A tool for environmental improvement," *Total Quality Environmental Management,* 5(1), Autumn, 35-49.

Klassen, R.D. (1993). "The integration of environmental issues into manufacturing: Toward an interactive open-systems model," *Production & Inventory Management Journal,* 34(1), First Quarter, 82-88.

Klassen, R.D. & McLaughlin, C.P. "TQM and environmental excellence in manufacturing," *Industrial Management and Data Systems,* 1993, 93(6), 14-22.

Klassen, R.D. & McLaughlin, C.P. "The impact of environmental management on firm performance," *Management Science,* 1996, 42(8), 1199-1214.

Kopicki, R.J., Legg, L.L., & Novak, K.E. "Reuse and recycling: Reverse logistics opportunities," *Annual Conference Proceedings, Council of Logistics Management,* October 3-6, 1993, 29-36.

Leenders, M.R. & Fearon. H.E. *Purchasing and materials management,* Tenth Edition. Homewood: Richard D. Irwin, Inc., 1993.

Leenders, M., Nollet, J. and Ellram, L. (1994). "Adapting purchasing to supply chain management," *International Journal of Physical Distribution & Logistics Management,* 24(1), 40-42.

Livingstone, S. & Sparks, L. "The new German packaging laws: Effects on firms exporting to Germany," *International Journal of Physical Distribution and Logistics Management,* 1994, 24(7), 15-25.

McGuire, J.B, Sungren, A. & Schneeweis, T. "Corporate social responsibility and firm performance," *Academy of Management Journal,* 1988, 31(xxy), 854-872.

Miakisz, J.A. (1994). "Measuring environmental performance at Niagara Mohawk Power," *Total Quality Environmental Management,* 4(1), Autumn, 47-56.

Miles, M.B., and Huberman, A.M. (1984). *Qualitative data analysis: A source book of new methods.* Newbury Park, CA: Sage Publications.

Min, H. and Galle, W.P. (1997). "Green Purchasing Strategies: Trends and implications," *International Journal of Purchasing and Materials Management,* 33(3), 10-17.

Monczka, R.M. & Trent, R.J. *Purchasing and sourcing strategy: Trends and implications.* Tempe: Center For Advanced Purchasing Studies, 1995.

Morton, R.R. (1994). "Using GEMI's environmental self-assessment procedure (ESAP) to evaluate environmental performance," *Total Quality Environmental Management,* 4(1), Autumn, 75-83.

Murphy, P.R., Poist, R.F., & Braunschwieg, C.D. "Management of environmental issues in logistics: Current status and future potential," *Transportation Journal,* 1994, 34(1), 48-56.

Murphy, P.R., Poist, R.F., & Braunschwieg, C.D. "Role and relevance of logistics to corporate environmentalism: An empirical assessment," *International Journal of Physical Distribution and Logistics Management,* 1995, 25(2), 5-19.

Novartis, (1992) *Guide to risk analysis,* Ciba-Giegy Limited, Corporate Safety and Environmental, and Novartis Communications, Basel, Switzerland.

O Dea, K. and Pratt, K. (1995). "Achieving environmental excellence through TQEM strategic alliances," *Total Quality Environmental Management,* 4(3), Spring, 93-108.

Oakley, B.T. (1993). "Total quality product design - How to integrate environmental criteria into the production realization process," *Total Quality Environmental Management,* 2(3), Spring, 309-321.

Paton, B. (1993). "Environmentally conscious product design through total quality management," *Total Quality Environmental Management,* 2(4), Summer, 383-396.

Pohlen, T.L. & Farris II, M.T. "Reverse logistics in plastics recycling," *International Journal of Physical Distribution and Logistics Management,* 1992, 22(7), 35.

Porter, M.E. *Competitive Advantage,* New York: The Free Press, 1985.

Porter, M.E. and van der Linde, C. (1995). "Green and competitive: Ending the stalemate," *Harvard Business Review,* September-October, 120-134.

Porter, M.E. & van der Linde, C. "Toward a new conception of the environment-competitiveness relationship," *Journal of Economic Perspectives,* 1995 9(4), 97-118.

Rice, F. "Who scores best on the environment," *Fortune,* July 26, 1993, 114-118.

Rodenhurst, G. and Spens, C. (1993). "Supporting TQEM with Boeing's environmental assessment monitoring program," *Total Quality Environmental Management,* 2(3), Spring, 291-296.

Sarkis, J. (1995)."Manufacturing strategy and environmental consciousness," *Technovation,* 15(2) 79-97.

Scott, C. and Westbrook, R. (1991). "New strategic tools for supply chain management," *International Journal of Physical Distribution & Logistics Management,* 23-33.

Shimwell, P. "Corporate environmental policy in practice," *Long Range Planning,* 1991, 24(3), 10-17.

Shrivastava, P., & Hart, S. "Greening organizations — 2000," *International Journal of Public Administration,* 1994, 17(3,4), 607-635.

Sullivan, M.S. and Ehrenfeld, J.R. (1992). "Reducing life-cycle environmental impacts: An industry survey of emerging tools and programs," *Total Quality Environmental Management,* 2(2), Winter, 143-157.

Tibor, T. & Feldman, *I. ISO 14000: A guide to the new environmental management standards.* Chicago: Irwin, 1996.

Thompson, B.C and Rauck, A.C. (1993). "Applying TQEM practices to pollution prevention at AT&T's Columbus Works plant," *Total Quality Environmental Management,* 2(4), Summer, 373-381.

Turner, J.R. (1993). "Integrated supply chain management: What's wrong with this picture?" *Industrial Engineering,* December, 52-55.

Walley, N. & Whitehead, B. "It's not easy being green," *Harvard Business Review,* 1994 (May-June), 46-52.

Weissman, S.H. and Sekutowski, J.C. (1991). "Environmentally conscious manufacturing," AT&T *Technical Journal,* 70(6), 23-30.

Wever, G.H and Vorhauer, G.F., (1993). "Kodak's framework and assessment tool for implementing TQEM," *Total Quality Environmental Management,* 3(1), Autumn, 19-30.

Wheeler, W.A., (1992) "The revival in reverse manufacturing," *Journal of Business Strategy,* 13(4), 8-13.

Winsemius, P. & Guntram U. "Responding to the environmental challenge," *Business Horizons,* 1992 (March-April), 12-20.

Wise, G. L. (1995) "Ciba-Geigy develops new regional remediation teams to manage Superfund programs," *Total Quality Environmental Management,* 4(3), Spring, 21-32.

Wolfe, A. and Howes, H.A. (1993). "Measuring environmental performance: Theory and practice at Ontario Hydro," *Total Quality Environmental Management,* 2(4), Summer, 355-366.

Wu, H. J., and Dunn, S. C. (1995). "Environmentally responsible logistics systems," *International Journal of Physical Distribution & Logistics Management,* 25(2), 20-38.

CENTER FOR ADVANCED PURCHASING STUDIES •

THE CENTER FOR ADVANCED PURCHASING STUDIES (CAPS) was established in November 1986 as the result of an affiliation agreement between the College of Business at Arizona State University and the National Association of Purchasing Management. It is located at The Arizona State University Research Park, 2055 East Centennial Circle, P.O. Box 22160, Tempe, Arizona 85285-2160 (Telephone [602] 752-2277).

The Center has three major goals to be accomplished through its research program:

to improve purchasing effectiveness and efficiency;
to improve overall purchasing capability;
to increase the competitiveness of U.S. companies in a global economy.

Research published includes 33 focus studies on purchasing/materials management topics ranging from purchasing organizational relationships to CEOs' expectations of the purchasing function, as well as benchmarking reports on purchasing performance in 26 industries.

Research under way includes: *Major Changes in Purchasing/Supply Organizations; Managing the Year 2000 Supplier Compliance Process; International Purchasing and Supply Management in the United States and in Germany;* and the benchmarking reports of purchasing performance by industry.

CAPS, affiliated with two 501 (c) (3) educational organizations, is funded solely by tax-deductible contributions from organizations and individuals who want to make a difference in the state of purchasing and materials management knowledge. Policy guidance is provided by the Board of Trustees consisting of: